THE GARDEN IN WINTER

D1396431

Pan Piper Small Garden Series
Editor: C. E. Lucas Phillips

THE GARDEN IN WINTER

MINA SMITH

with illustrations by the author

PAN BOOKS LTD · LONDON

First published 1966 by Museum Press Ltd.
This edition published 1969 by Pan Books Ltd,
33 Tothill Street, London, S.W.1

330 02381 0

Printed in Great Britain by
Cox & Wyman Ltd., London, Reading and Fakenham

CONTENTS

Chapter One

Attractions of the Winter Garden

The first sharp frost of the season changes every garden and
when summer gives way to autumn overnight we may feel
either pleasure or nostalgia depending upon the kind of garden
we own. Dahlias hanging blackened on their stems can strike a
chill deeper than frost itself into the hearts of 'summer only'
gardeners, but to those who plan for year-round enjoyment
the sight is not so sad. Dahlias are scarcely missed when our
eyes can rest on true autumn flowers, on rich leaf colour, or on
gleaming berries, and there are so many plants with these
good qualities that it is difficult to choose between them. Such
a blaze of autumn colour is certainly a desirable target but
garden beauty need not end with the falling leaves. The
character of the garden must alter in winter but it can be
just as attractive.

First impressions of summer gardens are usually hazy ones,
dominated by amorphous masses or colour. The impact made
by a pleasant winter garden is quite different. It is definite and
cleancut, relying more on shape than on colour to catch the
eye. Colour is still important but it is usually more subdued,
or else it appears in small dots and patches of brilliance rather
than in any large expanse. Some of the brightest colours are
provided by the many berries and other fruits which are
retained for a long time after leaf-fall and look exceedingly
decorative on otherwise bare twigs. Then later, in the very
bleakest months, winter-blooming plants astound us with the
hardiness of their fragile-seeming flowers. Nor are these the
only beauties of the winter garden. A number of trees and
shrubs can be admired for their stem colour, others for the
grace of their spire-like or weeping silhouettes, while furry,

1. Colourful autumn fruits, *Callicarpa bodinieri giraldii* and (in front) *Euonymus europaeus,* the spindle-tree

evergreen conifers contrast well with the lacy patterns made by the twigs of deciduous trees. We can appreciate these and many other shapes in winter when the bare bones of the garden are revealed and we notice outlines which are hidden during the summer months.

Evergreens planted as hedges or in groups make splendid

protective screens and I have made some suggestions for using them like this in Chapter Eight. Evergreens, however, can play a much larger part in furnishing the garden in winter and they do not deserve to be dismissed as useful but uninspiring background subjects. Too many people imagine 'evergreen' to mean 'dull' and this is a pity, because interesting and beautiful evergreens far outnumber the dull ones. It will be seen from the descriptions of plants in Chapters Three to Six that evergreens grow in all shapes and sizes, from tall trees to prostrate, ground-covering plants. Many of them carry attractive flowers or fruits and the colour range of their foliage goes far beyond green. Some have golden leaves and some are red- or copper-tinged. Grey-leaved evergreens vary from pure silver to blue and there are other handsome kinds with glossy, variegated foliage that looks gay and bright in the dreariest weather.

Winter flowers, of course, are the jewels of the garden and, although they are less numerous than their summer cousins, they are not too difficult to grow or to find. Most all-round nurserymen include in their lists winter-blooming shrubs, bulbs, and herbaceous plants. It would be a very wealthy as well as a very clever gardener who could boast a show of flowers in January to equal that of July but for quite a modest sum we can have at least one kind of flower blooming out-of-doors in every month of the year.

The choice of a winter-blooming plant often starts us thinking about how to create a suitable setting for it and leads us to make the garden more attractive generally. We may decide to put the new treasure close to a sheltered seat that will tempt us to leave the fireside on bright days, or perhaps we decide to plant it near the house, where it can be seen from a window by those who are unable to go out.

All kinds of improvements suggest themselves once we begin to think about using the garden all the year round and from what I have said so far it will be plain that in order to enjoy a beautiful winter garden we have first of all to lay rather careful plans. These include making the most of our garden's contours and taking advantage of all the clean-cut, contrasting shapes and high-lights of colour that are available for blending

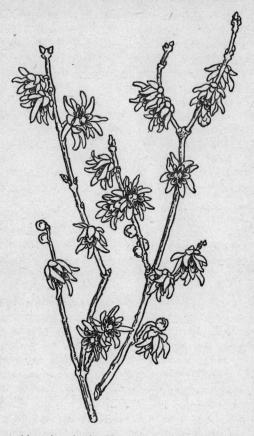

2. A winter-blooming shrub, *Chimonanthus praecox*, the winter-sweet

together into a pleasing picture. We must also remember that, although in summer Dame Nature may draw a flowery veil over the worst of our blunders and omissions, in winter she is in a less kindly mood and so we should be prepared to work harder to achieve the effects we want.

Another marked difference between the summer and the winter garden is the need for shelter. In summer this amounts to providing a shady spot for lazing when the sun is hottest, but during the winter months both people and plants find the garden an uncomfortable place without efficient windbreaks such as walls, fences, and hedges thoughtfully placed to baffle the wind while allowing every available blink of sunshine to reach the garden. A seat under cover and with a pleasant outlook is also much appreciated during the winter, at times when the weather is bad, or when we simply feel disinclined for active gardening.

THE SCOPE OF THIS BOOK

This book has been designed to help people who would like to make their gardens just as attractive in winter as they are in summer. Because we cannot influence the weather, I have dealt with clothes for the winter gardener in the next chapter, before going on to plants and planting. The following chapters give descriptions of a large number of plants which all have something to commend them during the darker months of the year.

I have not tried to give exact dates when individual plants make their peak contribution to garden beauty, because this varies with the weather and with the situation of the garden where the plants are grown. In Britain summer lasts longest in the south, and, at the other end of the calendar, signs of spring in southern gardens are usually two or three weeks ahead of those in the north. There are marked differences, too, between growing conditions in the east and in the west. Plants living near our western coasts often outstrip those grown in the chillier eastern districts, both in general wellbeing and in earliness of bloom.

Nor is it possible to say exactly how long coloured leaves or fruit will remain on the branches, because the performance of most plants in this respect varies from year to year. It is influenced by all kinds of things, such as the amounts of sunshine and rain during the growing season, autumn winds and temperatures, and the attentions of birds and insects. The age of plants can make a difference too, young trees and shrubs often retaining their foliage longer than mature specimens of the same variety. But these are not serious drawbacks to planning. It is easy enough to discover at which season plants are most decorative and one of the pleasures of gardening is in finding out how our own specimens behave and in making the most of local conditions.

Chapters Seven and Eight give some suggestions for the siting and construction of paths, walls, fences, and hedges. A garden without these amenities is unlikely to be a success and would certainly not be enjoyed in winter. After planning a protective framework for our plants, we naturally want to see them looking their best, so ideas on garden layout will be found in Chapters Nine and Ten. They include plant groupings and suggestions for combining these with structural features such as sheltered seats, statues, and pools to make the winter garden both interesting and beautiful.

Chapters Eleven and Twelve should be particularly helpful to inexperienced gardeners. They deal with the choice of suitable plants for different localities, with soil preparation, and with the planting and aftercare of new stock. The last chapter is a general one on some of the routine tasks occurring in winter. It includes compost-making after the autumn clean-up and collection of fallen leaves, the care of garden furniture, what to do about ice on pools and snow on plants, preparations for new lawns and the improvement of established ones, and, lastly, some notes about feeding the wild birds who live in our gardens or who visit them during hard weather.

Chapter Two

Clothes for the Winter Gardener

The clothes we wear for gardening in winter should be suitable both for the time of year and for our activities. We cannot enjoy ourselves for long if our feet are cold or wet, if we feel cold generally, if our fingers are numb, or if we are so tightly bundled up that movement is difficult.

Some people have no choice but to wear stout leather boots or shoes at all times, and, provided they also wear reasonably thick socks and keep away from puddles, their feet should be perfectly warm and dry out of doors. Rubber boots are the only completely waterproof footwear, however, and those of us who do not need the firmer support of leather will find them excellent for the garden, particularly the cheaper boots which are very light in weight. Tight rubber boots are not comfortable because they make our feet very cold. They should be large enough for two pairs of socks to be worn inside (or socks over stockings) and still have room for us to wriggle our toes.

Slacks are warm and they are suitable for both men and women engaged in active outdoor work, but not all women like to wear them. Those who dislike slacks will find wool or nylon tights a practical alternative, worn with an ordinary skirt.

Some kind of coat or jacket is nearly always needed for gardening in winter and one with roomy pockets is the most useful as it can take the place of a gardener's apron to hold string, secateurs, and other bits and pieces.

Generally, we are more comfortable inside several loose lightweight layers of clothing than in a single thick tight one. For energetic work such as digging two thin jerseys under a

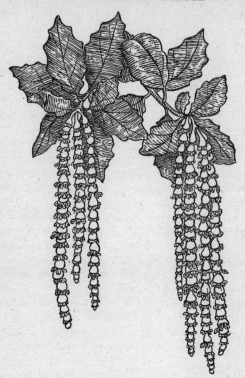

3. A catkin-bearing, evergreen shrub, *Garrya elliptica*

shower-proof jacket give much more freedom than one excessively heavy jersey or coat. We can peel off our top clothes
like onion skins, one layer at a time, as the work warms us,
and we will not catch cold if we remember to put them on again
when we stop digging and sit down to rest or change to a more
passive task.

Thin plastic raincoats are cheap, they keep one dry, and they
make good wind-cheaters when standing or sitting still, but
they have several disadvantages for wear in the garden.
Although they stop the force of the wind, these coats will not

keep out the cold unless they are large enough to cover adequate jerseys or other warm clothes. They also tear very easily indeed, and, if worn for active work, their lack of ventilation soon makes one uncomfortably hot and damp.

Garden gloves are sensible wear at all times of year and particularly so in winter when they not only protect our hands from thorns, dirt, and rough surfaces, but prevent them becoming chapped. The leather gloves sold specially for heavy outdoor work are often too stiff to be comfortable, but ordinary leather gloves are quite good and a pair which has become too shabby for street wear will last a long time in the garden, because even thin leather is tough. Woollen gloves are not much use, they catch on snags and soon become wet through. Rubberized or vinyl-impregnated fabric gloves are probably the best for general garden work, and they are much superior to unlined rubber gloves which can make our hands either cold or sweaty. No matter what material we choose for gloves, the right size is important. In too large gloves we are clumsy, while in tight gloves our hands become numb with cold.

Such tasks as the tying-in of prickly shoots call for protection and neat finger work and then mittens are handy if we intend to keep both our skins and our tempers intact. Old leather gloves with about a third of each finger cut off make serviceable mittens.

I have thought for a long time that men were very scurvily treated in the matter of winter headgear, with their poor red ears exposed to all weathers, but now that their fashions are breaking away from the old conventions it should soon be possible for the male winter gardener to take refuge inside a tied-down deerstalker without causing too much of a stir.

Women are much luckier because there is nothing quite so successful for keeping out the cold as a head scarf tied cosily over the ears. It makes almost as much difference as warm gloves to whether or not we feel comfortable in the winter garden. Woollen or other matt-surfaced scarves are the best for staying in place. Silk scarves have an irritating trick of sliding off and letting hair blow in our eyes when both our hands are full. And if we want to be a little more stylish we can wear the scarf tied over a small hat.

Another part of men's conventional clothing, the collar and tie, can cause trouble to the winter gardener, not while they are being worn but when they are discarded in favour of an open-necked shirt. This often leads to chills and sore throats, so it is better to tuck a scarf into the neck of the shirt or to wear a high-necked pullover.

Although not strictly clothing, a waterproof kneeling pad can also add to our comfort and help us to avoid chills. A piece of foam rubber answers very well, or a firm cushion slipped inside a polythene bag. With this to complete our winter outfit there is every chance of enjoying quite long spells in the garden during cold weather.

Chapter Three

Autumn Flowers

The first step we can take towards making our gardens attractive all the year round is to prolong the flowering season of some of the plants which bloom in summer and, when there is a choice, to include late-blooming varieties among them. Plants grown in well-cultivated ground and kept supplied with water during dry spells continue to bloom longer than plants growing under less favourable conditions; so good soil preparation, watering, feeding, and mulching all affect the performance of our plants. A great many plants, too, will bloom longer if they are prevented from setting seed, and the prompt removal of faded flowers is a big help towards maintaining a colourful garden.

HERBACEOUS PLANTS

My own favourites among the plants which keep going from summer into autumn are the lavender *Scabiosa caucasica*, 'Clive Greaves', with its round, pincushioned-centred blooms, and the hybrid aquilegias, those long-spurred and many-coloured columbines whose flowers are delicate as butterflies. I also like the pink and white daisies of *Erigeron mucronatus*, a determined little plant about nine inches high which sets a great deal of seed and pops up in odd places.

Anthemis cupaniana is a rather larger and bolder-looking daisy with pure white yellow-eyed flowers. Belonging to the chamomile family it has low-growing, grey-green aromatic foliage which looks pretty on the rockery. Another plant with a long flowering season is the prostrate evening primrose, *Oenothera missouriensis*. It has large, silky, yellow flowers and I

4. *Dianthus* 'Prudence'

have seen it blooming at Wisley in the middle of November.

The hybrid pinks gratefully repay regular summer feeding by blooming all through the autumn. Three delightful varieties are *Dianthus* 'Doris', salmon-pink, *D.* 'Prudence', pink laced with wine-purple, and *D.* 'Wink', pure white with a small green eye.

Very different from the tidy and well-behaved pinks are two eupatoriums, American relatives of our native hemp-agrimony. These coarse long-blooming plants are most at home in the wild garden. *E. ageratoides*, with terminal heads of white flowers, grows about three feet tall and *E. purpureum*, with deep purple flowers, reaches five feet. Both bloom from August until the end of October in moist soil.

Turning to the bright, warm colours connected in our minds with autumn, the geums, although mainly summer-flowering, will go on opening a few brilliant little scarlet, orange or yellow faces for a long time if they are not allowed to seed. These plants grow about two feet tall. The semi-double 'Lady Stratheden' is not only a handsome variety but one of the most hard working and produces batches of frilly golden flowers until autumn is well advanced.

Inula royleana is another border plant growing two feet tall. It has shaggy orange daisy flowers from July to October.

Gaillardias and heleniums are two very-well-liked and reliable border plants. They bloom from midsummer onwards and their velvety yellow, red, and brown daisy flowers blend with the first ripening berries and tinted leaves of autumn. The most characteristic of the gaillardias, growing about two feet tall, have target-like flowers with zones of two and three colours in one bloom. Heleniums, growing three to four feet tall, have rather reflexed petals and conspicuous domed centres to the flowers. 'July Sun' is bright yellow with a dark brown centre, 'Moerheim Beauty' is mahogany-red and 'Riverton Gem' is terra-cotta streaked with gold.

Some of the rudbeckias, or coneflowers, reach five or six feet in height and their golden-yellow faces stare at us from August until October. 'Goldsturm', often called 'Black-Eyed Susan', is a radiant, late-blooming variety with high, black 'cones' in the centre of its flowers. 'Herbstsonne' is another fine variety with green 'cones'.

Echinacea 'The King' is a close relative of the rudbeckias with very striking red-purple flowers. Another royal-sounding daisy is *Helianthus* 'Monarch', a perennial sunflower which can grow a good deal more than six feet tall and has showy flowers of brightest sunshine-yellow.

But not all the autumn-blooming herbaceous plants have round flowers; there are many with tall spikes of bloom and these make a pleasant contrast in form. Several kniphofias, the red-hot-pokers, bloom late in the season. They include the dwarf *K. galpinii*, with yellowish-orange flowers, *K. snowdeni*, coral-red, 'Royal Standard', in the traditional red-hot-poker colours of yellow below and scarlet above, and the lovely 'Maid of Orleans' which is ivory-white.

The kniphofias like sunshine and, for growing in shady places, the less substantial creamy spikes of cimicifuga are very attractive with their bead-like buds and with their fluffy flowers opening in succession for a long time.

Solidago, the golden-rod, provides bright yellow, branching spikes for the late summer and autumn garden. Some of the newer hybrids are more interesting and less invasive than the older types, but for late bloom the tall 'Golden Wings' is still popular although it gained an award of merit as long ago as 1907. Just in front of this solidago is a good position for the all-red cardinal-flower, *Lobelia cardinalis* 'Queen Victoria' which has beetroot-crimson foliage and scarlet flowers. These begin to open in mid-summer but continue until the end of October, so the plant can glow on its own until the golden-rod is ready to bloom and then join it in a fine blaze of red and gold.

Blue and lavender flowers cool down these fiery colours and make a useful barrier between them and the softer pinks or pinky-mauves which are still plentiful at the end of summer. Delphiniums from which the early blooms were removed will supply a second crop of flowers on their side-shoots and the cool sky-blues are, I think, the loveliest of all to contrast with full-blooded autumn colours. Aconitum, the monk's-hood, although less tall and showy than the delphinium, is its late summer counterpart. *A. fischeri* is a particularly late-blooming species with many light violet-blue helmet-shaped flowers in terminal spikes. It grows three feet tall and likes a damp and slightly shady spot best of all.

For a position in full sun *Salvia uliginosa*, growing about four feet tall, provides spikes of pale blue flowers. These are quaintly shaped too, with widely opened lips, and they come out a few at a time from August until very late in the autumn. *Physostegia* 'Vivid', the 'obedient plant', provides us with rosy-mauve spikes of bloom over the same long period and is quite happy in similar conditions so, being only half as tall, it can be grown in front of the salvia. *Liatris spicata* has deeper rosy-purple blooms in fluffy spikes but it does not last quite so long and sometimes looks bedraggled because the flowers open from the top of the spikes downwards.

On the rock garden one of the longest blooming plants is *Polygonum affine*, with short spikes of deep rose or crimson flowers appearing above its dense mats of foliage all through the summer and autumn. Even then the display is not over, for the foliage turns coppery-red in winter and the flower spikes remain as decorative brown seed heads. An utterly different long-blooming plant for the rockery is the low-growing *Campanula poscharskyana*, with lavender-blue or white starry flowers appearing from June until October. *Zauchneria californica* is a late-blooming rock plant to keep these two company. It is a shrubby plant and in September and October the hairy, grey-green foliage is covered with tubular flowers of the brightest scarlet.

Michaelmas-daisies are one of the glories of the autumn borders, exploding with a thousand stars in September and October and including in their colour range all the purples and all the pinks, blues, and reds that contain a hint of violet. Most of the gorgeous large-flowered Michaelmas-daisies belong to the novi-belgii group of perennial asters, and there are far too many good varieties for any to be singled out here. The dwarf hybrid Michaelmas-daisies are equally showy and one of the latest of these to bloom must have a special mention. This is the delightful *A.* 'Blue Bouquet', which smothers itself in bright, lavender-blue flowers and still looks fresh as paint at the end of October, when it proves a great attraction to butterflies. *A. cordifolius* and *A. ericoides* are plants with an entirely different charm. Both have long, graceful arching sprays of tiny, pastel-coloured daisies and because of their very daintiness are inclined to be overlooked in favour of the bolder kinds.

Elegant plants which associate well with these small-flowered asters are the Japanese anemones, to be found in catalogues under *Anemone hybrida*, *A. hupehensis*, or (incorrectly) *A. japonica*. These pure white or pink anemones have shallow, cup-shaped blooms with perfectly round green centres and rich

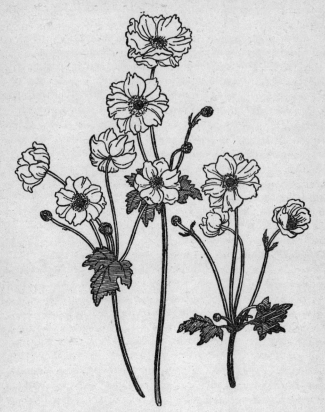

5. *Anemone hupehensis*, a Japanese anemone

golden stamens. I like the colour combination best in the white flowers and think the pink and yellow clash, but this is a small fault to set against the grace and style of the whole plant, which grows about three feet tall and carries its flowers proudly at the ends of slender stems. The Japanese anemones begin to open before the Michaelmas-daisies and go on blooming for some time after these have finished.

The hardy chrysanthemums form another most important

group of true autumn flowers and the most remarkable for massed colour and lateness of bloom are the Korean and pom-pom chrysanthemums. The Otley Korean chrysanthemums are a well-known strain of plants, which form rounded hummocks of foliage and then hide them under flowers in the manner of the dwarf hybrid Michaelmas-daisies but in a wider colour range of mauves, pinks, yellows, and reds that includes some mouth-watering apricots, tans, and coppery-browns. The latest-blooming Koreans are all rather taller plants than these, reaching about three feet in height. 'Eve' has semi-double, brick-red flowers, 'Rosalie' has red buds opening to single pink flowers, and 'Wedding Day' has single, white, green-eyed flowers. The pom-pom chrysanthemums are almost indistinguishable from some pom-pom dahlias but, unlike the dahlias, they are unharmed by frost. There are several good pinks and whites among them; 'Bob' is a striking bright red and 'Jante Wells', the best known of all small chrysanthemums, has sunshine-yellow flowers.

Chrysanthemum uliginosum is a vastly different plant which grows five feet tall and has flat, white flowers with greenish-yellow centres. This is the 'giant ox-eye daisy', an easy-going country bumpkin of a plant compared with the spruce and highly bred chrysanthemums I have just mentioned. It blooms all through September and October and looks very well in a mixed border.

Coming right down to ground level again *Convolvulus mauritanicus* is a pretty little plant which creeps along opening its wide, violet-blue flowers from late summer until November. As it is not at all aggressive, in spite of its bindweed blood, this convolvulus can be allowed to ramble about as the fancy takes it. The nine-inch high *Ceratostigma plumbaginoides*, which produces its vivid blue phlox-like flowers at about the same time, is much less to be trusted, and it is only tolerated in some gardens for the richness of its autumn colouring when the foliage reddens and makes such a fine background for the flowers. *Clematis heracleifolia* is a shrubby, three-foot high plant producing a great many clusters of small blue flowers in the leaf axils during late summer and autumn.

6. *Gentiana acaulis*

But when we begin to consider blue flowers for the autumn garden everything pales before *Gentiana sino-ornata*. This incomparable plant grows no more than four inches high, holding up its gorgeous trumpets on short leafy stems and when growing conditions are to its liking forming pools of the deepest blue imaginable. It begins to bloom in early autumn and may continue until Christmas if the weather is good. This gentian must have lime-free soil. Those whose gardens are limy, however, can still try *G. sino-ornata* because it is not a very big plant and can be accommodated in small beds or pockets filled with suitably peaty soil and walled with polythene to prevent seepage from the surrounding ground. It can also be grown in troughs and sinks if these are kept moist by being buried almost to their rims in the ground.

Gentiana acaulis is a spring-blooming plant, very similar to *G. sino-ornata*, and it often blooms for a second time in autumn, so if we cannot please *G. sino-ornata* we can try our luck with this gentian instead. I have also looked enviously at the clear sky-blue trumpets of *G. farreri* blooming in Kew Gardens at the end of October, but this plant has such a reputation for being an awkward customer that I have not been brave enough to buy it.

Leaving the sumptuous blue gentians, we have for contrast a pretty pink-flowered plant which obligingly blooms in spring and again in autumn. This is *Heucherella* 'Bridget Bloom', with many eighteen-inch stems of tiny flowers. The heucherellas are hybrids between species of *Heuchera*, the popular alumroot, and *Tiarella*, the foam-flower, and take after both dainty parents.

Saxifraga fortunei is a true autumn-blooming plant, with panicles of fragile, moth-like flowers fluttering above a tuft of rounded leaves. This saxifrage is hardy and grows about a foot tall. It does well in slight shade and, as the white flowers can be spoilt by frost, they last best under the protection of overhanging branches, provided these are not too dense.

Hosta tardiflora also enjoys slight shade and is about the same height. It has a clump of dark-green, leathery leaves, from which spikes of down-pointed, pale-lavender bells rise in September and October. *H. tardiflora* is the last of its very decorative genus to bloom.

Liriope muscari is a little taller but, like the hosta, it forms a clump of foliage and in autumn sends up its flower spikes. The small flowers are lavender-blue and bead-like. They cluster tightly along the slender stems and really do resemble the spring-flowering muscari from which this plant takes its name.

For another change of form several plants related to the cornflowers will make a good autumn show in a sunny place. *Centaurea dealbata* grows two feet high and its rosy-mauve flowers contrast well with the grey-green foliage. *Stokesia cyanea* has lavender-blue flowers and is about half the height of the centaurea, while *Serratula shawii* is a more delicately formed little plant less than a foot tall. Its mauve flowers resemble small thistles and the stiff, deeply cut foliage takes on purplish-bronze autumn tints.

7. *Saxifraga fortunei*

Sedum spectabile is a massive stonecrop growing eighteen inches high. Its stout upright stems are dressed in tidily arranged fleshy leaves and crowned with flat heads of close-packed pink flowers. The flowers come out in early autumn and at that time they attract crowds of butterflies, but the plant's contribution to the garden scene does not end there. Later the faded flowers turn a reddish-brown and remain colourful all winter. 'Autumn Joy' and 'Ruby Glow' are very fine newcomers, richly coloured.

A striking and long-lasting plant of quite a different kind is the stately pampas-grass, *Cortaderia argentea*, whose white plumes open in autumn and, like the flowers of *Sedum spectabile*, last all through the winter. This giant grass can form a tuft of foliage more than twelve feet across, with flower spikes nine feet high, but there is a smaller form, *C. a.*

'Pumila', which is easier to fit into most gardens, as it is only four to five feet tall and proportionally less spreading.

BULBS

Coming now to bulbous plants, it seems only fair to mention the 'Autumn-crocus' first and that immediately lands us in a state of confusion, because the plant commonly called the autumn-crocus is not a crocus but a *Colchicum*, although there are genuine autumn-blooming crocuses as well. *Colchicum autumnale*, the so-called autumn-crocus or meadow-saffron, is one of our native plants and is still found locally in south-east England. Its other common name of 'naked ladies' is very apt when we see the pale mauve crocus-like flowers appearing without a stitch of foliage in September. *C. speciosum* 'Album' is another lovely plant, with very fine white flowers, rather taller and more solid than *C. autumnale*. Corms of these and several other species are usually obtainable and there are many beautiful garden hybrids. The leaves of colchicums are nine inches or more long and they appear in late spring. When the corms are planted in summer we have to remember this, and allow room for the foliage to mature without harming small plants nearby.

Of the true autumn-flowering crocuses, *C. kotschyanus* (*zonatus*) appears first, with the pale, rosy-lilac flowers coming before the leaves. *C. speciosus* follows it and this lovely little crocus has a number of varieties which give it a colour range from pure white to deepest violet and a season of bloom lasting from September until November. There are many other autumn-flowering crocuses, but these two species are particularly easy and free flowering.

Two other crocus-like plants for the autumn garden are *Sternbergia lutea* and *Zephyranthes candida*. *Sternbergia lutea angustifolia* is the most free-blooming form, with many bright-yellow flowers in September and October. The zephyranthes produces pure white blooms at the same time of year and both plants need a really warm and sunny spot and a gritty soil if they are to do well.

Amaryllis belladonna, the belladonna-lily, is a magnificent early autumn flower but a temperamental one, with clusters of large, sweet-scented rose-pink trumpets on stout stems eighteen inches or more high. This plant insists upon the hottest and driest spot in the garden, with shelter behind it, but even then it may not condescend to bloom.

For a reliable, pink-flowered bulbous plant we do better to choose *Nerine bowdenii*. This also likes a sunny and well drained spot but it never sulks and produces its delightful peppermint-pink heads of bloom every autumn without fail.

Schizostylis coccinea, the Kaffir-lily, has spikes of rosy-red flowers in autumn and early winter. Like the last two bulbs mentioned the schizostylis comes from South Africa, so it enjoys sunshine, but is also needs plenty of moisture during the growing season. The flower spikes are like those of the gladiolus in construction but the flowers themselves resemble crocuses. 'Mrs Hegarty' and *S. c.* 'Viscountess Byng' are two equally lovely pink varieties.

There are many species of hardy cyclamen growing only a few inches tall and it is possible to have the different sorts blooming continuously from August until April although some are too expensive to be risked outside and usually live in the safety of alpine houses. *C. neapolitanum* is happily not one of these, so it can be planted in drifts to provide rose-pink flowers from September to November and a beautiful ground cover of dark green, marbled leaves all through the winter. *C. n. album* is a white variety with even more handsome leaves. *C. cilicium* is a species with pale pink flowers. It shares *C. neapolitanum*'s liking for growing under deciduous trees and blooms at much the same time. All the hardy cyclamen prefer limy to acid soil and like a well-drained spot.

The next two bulbs I am going to suggest may seem a little unseasonable, but for those gardeners who do not feel they are out of place here are two autumn-blooming snowdrops. *Galanthus nivalis reginae-olgae* begins to bloom in October and *G. corcyrensis* in November. Unlike the 'fair maids of February', these snowdrops both need a sunny position, and, as they only grow three to four inches high, they need a safe

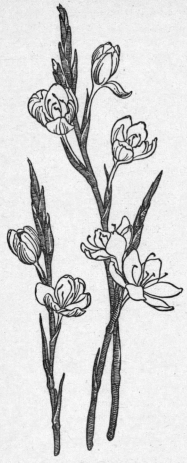

8. *Schizostylis coccinea*, the Kaffir-lily

corner where they will not be smothered by taller plants.

Leucojum autumnale, the autumn snowflake, is another dainty
little bulb which blooms in September and October and its
small white bells on thread-like stems make it look even more
of a fragile fairy-flower than the snowdrops.

SHRUBS

Not many shrubs begin to flower in autumn but there are a few, and as a great many summer-flowering kinds continue well into this season there is no need for a gap before the early winter show is ready.

The hybrid-tea roses are autumn- as well as summer-blooming and many of the shrub roses which bloom again late in the year give us the pleasant sight of flowers and fruit appearing together. The China and Bourbon roses are particularly generous with both the quantity and the quality of their autumn flowers.

Potentillas are undoubtedly the best shrubs for continuous bloom throughout the summer and autumn and this is not their only attraction. They have neat and pretty foliage, while their flowers, which are like small wild roses, can be obtained in all the yellows from pale cream to a deep orangey egg-yolk colour. *Potentilla fruticosa* 'Katherine Dykes', with sulphur-yellow flowers, makes a stout bush four feet high or rather more. *cc* "Vilmoriniana" is a little less tall and is very beautiful, with silvery-grey foliage and cream flowers, while 'Moonlight' is shorter still and has pale yellow flowers. There are also low-growing, almost prostrate potentillas which look handsome in the rock garden.

The hypericums, or St John's worts, are also yellow-flowered shrubs with a long season of bloom. The most outstanding is the evergreen *Hypericum patulum* 'Hidcote' which makes a bush up to six feet tall. The saucer-shaped, buttercup-yellow flowers have conspicuous centres set in a ring of deeper gold stamens.

A lovely companion for this hypericum is *Romneya coulteri*, the Californian tree-poppy. This is a rather tender shrub belonging to the poppy family. The foliage is bluish-green and the flowers are large, with pure white, pleated and goffered petals, round massed golden stamens. They are very similar to the flowers of the herbaceous oriental poppies blooming in early summer. *R. coulteri* needs a sunny spot where it will begin to bloom in midsummer and continue until October.

As a change from all these yellow and white flowers, we need

9. *Hypericum patulum* 'Hidcote' and (behind) *Ceratostigma willmottianum*

some blue in the shrub border and nothing could be more
suitable than *Ceratostigma willmottianum*, whose flowers are a
true blue and not just a 'catalogue' blue which so often turns
out to be only a purple patch. *C. willmottianum* is a dainty
little shrub with thin wiry stems. It grows about three feet
tall and the small leaves colour attractively before they fall.

The very bright blue flowers grow in tightly packed heads and open a few at a time on every sunny day, beginning in mid-summer and continuing through the autumn.

Caryopteris clandonensis is a somewhat taller shrub whose slender, arching stems carry many pairs of grey-green, aromatic leaves. The misty blue flowers appear in the leaf axils and come out mostly in August and September but they sometimes last into October. Both *Ceratostigma willmottianum* and *Caryopteris clandonensis* are hardy, although their top growth may be cut back by frost.

The ceanothus are rather more delicate, blue-flowered shrubs, so in all but the most sheltered gardens they do best when protected by a wall. Many ceanothus are spring-blooming but others bloom in late summer and continue into autumn. Of these *C.* 'Autumn Blue' and *C. burkwoodii* are two popular evergreen plants which are turned into blue clouds by their abundant flowers and 'Gloire de Versailles' is a deciduous shrub with very sweet-scented flowers in large clusters. *C. burkwoodii* is the brightest coloured of the three but also the least hardy.

For clothing other walls, there are several good late-flowering climbing shrubs and perhaps the most welcome are the sweet-scented honeysuckles. *Lonicera periclymenum* 'Sero-tina', the late Dutch honeysuckle, is rather like the wild honeysuckle of the hedgerows but the flowers are more richly coloured, reddish-purple on the outside and yellow within. *L. japonica* 'Halliana' is a fast-growing, evergreen climber with smaller but equally sweet-scented flowers appearing in pairs all along the new wood. The flowers are pale cream to begin with and change to a yellowish-fawn.

Polygonum baldschuanicum, the so-called Russian vine, deserves a mention here as a non-stop flowering climber with innumerable panicles of pinkish-white flowers appearing from midsummer until late autumn. But this plant is the most rampant of climbing shrubs and not at all suitable for small gardens, or for any position where it can overpower weaker neighbours.

Another rampant climber is the cheerful *Senecio scandens*,

which produces a great many small, bright-yellow daisy-flowers in autumn. It is not so overwhelming as the Russian vine, however, and in cold districts usually dies right back after flowering.

Of very different character is *Abutilon megapotamicum*, an elegant, tender shrub suitable only for a warm wall and a position in full sun. When the plant is happily placed its slender shoots will grow six to eight feet high and the quaint red and yellow tassel-like flowers will continue to appear until late autumn.

Several of the large-flowered clematis blooming in summer take a rest and then bloom again in autumn. 'The President' is one of these, with deep purple flowers. Others bloom tire-lessly from midsummer, never being completely without flowers until late in the autumn, although the last blooms are not always so colourful as the earlier ones. Two superb plants in this group are 'Beauty of Worcester', which has light violet flowers with prominent white stamens, and 'Ville de Lyon', a rich beetroot-red. *C. jouiniana* is a small-flowered hybrid clematis descended on one side from *C. vitalba*, the wild traveller's-joy of chalky districts. It looks rather like this parent except that the abundant flowers are white or violet-tinted instead of green. *C. jouiniana* begins to bloom in August and continues for about three months. *C. flammula*, the virgin's-bower, is another small-flowered climber with sweet-scented white blooms appearing over the same length of time, while *C. tangutica* is unusual among clematis in having yellow, lantern-like flowers.

Leaving the climbers and returning to the open border, *Phygelius capensis* 'Coccineus', the Cape-figwort, is a glowing red-flowered shrub. It has very large, branching flower heads, hung with quaint, curved buds, which open into hanging bells. This plant blooms best in light soil and in cold districts may be cut down by frost.

Hardy fuchsias also die back to ground level during the winter in cold districts, but they make strong growth again in spring and are ready to repeat their lasting display of red and purple bells in late summer and autumn. *Hebe* 'Autumn

Glory' is a shrubby veronica about two feet tall. The intense violet of its flowers looks very fine beside fuchsias and it is a stocky, free-flowering little bush for the autumn border. Both these shrubs do particularly well at the seaside and so do the escallonias, very beautiful glossy evergreens with masses of small pink or rich red trumpet flowers in summer and early autumn. The Donard strain of escallonias are particularly handsome plants, with larger flowers than the older kinds.

Those of us who garden on lime-free soil can plant heaths and heathers to provide massed colour in autumn. *Calluna vulgaris* is the common heather and there are many garden varieties of it which all bloom in autumn and have white, pink, mauve, wine-red or purple flowers. 'H. E. Beale' is a deservedly popular variety with long spikes of double rose-pink flowers. The colours of their evergreen foliage are very varied too, including gold, red, and many greens, so the heathers can be a most striking garden feature in suitable soil.

Daboecia cantabrica, the Irish heath, has an even longer flowering period than *Calluna vulgaris*, from June until November, and this plant can also be obtained in a number of distinct colours.

The ericas, or heaths, form the largest group among these three very similar genera and some, but by no means all, are autumn-flowering. Among the prettiest heaths for autumn bloom are the varieties of *Erica tetralix* with grey foliage and pink flowers. *E. terminalis*, the Corsican heath, will grow on limy soil and can be considered as part of the autumn show because the pink flowers which appear in late summer fade slowly to reddish-brown and remain decorative until the following spring. This is one of the larger heaths, reaching three feet or more in height.

The six-foot tall *Hydrangea paniculata* 'Grandiflora' which blooms in late summer and autumn, is useful in the same way as *Erica terminalis*. Its large conical heads of white flowers fade to pinkish-brown and look very striking after the foliage has fallen.

Arbutus unedo, the strawberry-tree, is an evergreen shrub

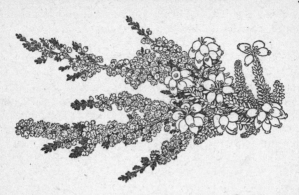

10. *Erica tetralix* and (behind) a double form of *Calluna vulgaris*

grown either as a large bush or in tree form. It has the unusual habit of blooming in autumn and at the same time producing fruits from the previous year's growth. The flowers of
the strawberry-tree are attractive waxy bells rather like lily-
of-the-valley but its knobbly red fruits are unfortunately not
strawberry-flavoured.

Although the mahonias are better known as foliage evergreens and winter-blooming shrubs, one handsome species is
obtainable which blooms from September to November. This
is *Mahonia fortunei*, a shrub reaching six feet in height and
having upright racemes of bright yellow flowers.

Another evergreen shrub which blooms in autumn is the
holly-like *Osmanthus illicifolius*. Its flowers are inconspicuous
but they are very fragrant and as there are several named
varieties of *O. illicifolius* with variegated foliage it pleases both
the eye and the nose.

Daphne mezereum 'Grandiflora' (*autumnalis*) is also a sweet-
scented shrub and the reddish-purple flowers clustered on its
stems begin to open in autumn and continue during mild
spells all winter.

Chapter Four

Autumn Leaves and Ornamental Fruits

The season of autumn leaf colour is the most variable and fleeting of all the garden's beauties. Plants which colour well in one district may remain comparatively dull in another, and, because of different weather, a particularly good or bad display during one autumn may not be repeated for several years. There are, however, many trees and shrubs whose foliage will colour well if conditions are right, so we can make a selection from these plants and the show they make in good seasons will compensate for an occasional disappointment.

Most striking of all are the trees and shrubs whose autumn leaves turn orange, flame, and red. Two which seem actually to catch fire are called, rather suitably, the smoke-trees, *Cotinus coggygria* (*Rhus cotinus*), and *Cotinus americanus* (*Rhus cotinoides*). Both make tall, spreading bushes closely covered with small rounded leaves and *C. coggygria* puffs out clouds of 'smoke' – billowing plumes of tiny pinkish flowers which turn grey just before the leaves colour. *Rhus typhina*, the stag's-horn sumach, is a relative of the smoke-trees and runs them close for flame-like colours. It is a tropical-looking tree, with very large leaves, divided into many pointed segments, and it grows well in towns.

The acers, or maples, are another group of trees with brilliantly coloured autumn leaves and these have the added attraction of being elegantly shaped. *Acer nikoense* has bright orange-red autumn leaves and *A. capillipes* has equally gorgeous leaves on pillar-box red stems. The foliage of *A. griseum*, the paperbark maple, turns to deeper but still vivid red, while its peeling trunk shows orange patches. A number of other maples grow into small, neat trees and colour splendidly in autumn. *A. palmatum* is the Japanese maple, often grown in rock gardens where it makes domes of dense, finely cut foliage. There are many varieties of *A. palmatum* with both green and bronze-red foliage and nearly all of them blaze up before the leaves fall.

Liquidambar styraciflua, the sweet-gum of North America, is a tall straight tree with foliage similar to the maples' and it colours as richly, the leaves adopting yellow, bright red, and purplish tints before settling for crimson.

Amelanchier canadensis, the snowy-mespilus, has come to us from America but it is a smaller tree, more like a cherry, with clouds of white blossom in April and oval leaves which turn to gold, orange, and coppery-red in autumn.

The ornamental cherries grown chiefly for their flowers in spring can put up a fine show of colour again in autumn. *Prunus avium*, the gean or wild cherry, changes its green dress for flame-red and reappears in the woods after being invisible since early summer. In the garden the leaves of many Japanese cherries turn gold and red before they fall and the incomparable *Prunus sargentii* positively glows. This is a tall, strong-growing tree which loads itself with pale pink flowers in spring.

Parrotia persica is a small tree or tall shrub whose hazel-like leaves turn to gold and then to bright red in autumn and before the winter is over its bare branches are clothed again with clusters of tiny red flowers.

Coming to smaller shrubs, many deciduous barberries are grown both for their berries and for their autumn leaf colour. *Berberis* 'Bountiful', 'Autumn Beauty', and 'Barbarossa', are just three from a long list of good plants whose tremendous crops of translucent red berries bend their arching stems and whose small neat leaves take on equally bright rich reds before they fall. *B. thunbergii* and its varieties make rather lower bushes and are less heavily berried but they are charmingly graceful shrubs and their autumn colours are outstanding, with hard sealing-wax red berries hanging among flame-red foliage. *B. wilsonae* is a still lower-growing barberry whose small, grey-green leaves turn purple, orange, and scarlet to

11. *Liquidambar styraciflua* and (in front) *Cotinus coggygria*

blend with the coral-red berries in a glorious mound of colour.
The cotoneasters are a huge genus of first-rate shrubs and
almost every garden we like to visit brings to light some fresh

12. *Berberis thunbergii*

species worth noting for its autumn colour. One which must be singled out is *Cotoneaster horizontalis*. This little shrub has bright red berries and richly varied autumn tints to add to the distinctive herring-bone pattern of its arching twigs. It can be allowed to creep over the ground or it can be trained to climb a wall and it is dainty enough to fit the smallest garden.

Our choice of fiery-leaved shrubs and trees is even wider where the soil is lime-free. Among the smaller bushes, deciduous azaleas and the very similar enkianthus become almost incandescent in suitable soils and so do the larger stuartias and oxydendrums which both thrive in conditions suitable for rhododendrons.

Nyssa sylvatica, a small tree with oval leaves rather like beech, and *Eucryphia glutinosa*, a large shrub with similar foliage, are two more plants with magnificent autumn colours in lime-free soil. The eucryphia is outstanding in midsummer too, when its white hypericum-like flowers are out.

The fothergillas also colour brilliantly in acid soil. Out of bloom the bushes look like witch-hazels but the white flowers appearing in late spring resemble very fluffy catkins or small bottle-brushes.

To even things up a bit for gardeners in chalky districts the leaves of the spindle trees, *Euonymus*, produce their lovely rose-madder autumn tints best in this kind of ground, while no one who has driven through Buckinghamshire on a late October day could fail to be impressed by the magnificence of the rust-red beech woods growing on shallow chalky soil. It takes a large garden to accommodate a fully grown beech tree, of course, but beech hedges can be kept as neat as privet and will retain their withered leaves all winter if they are trimmed in late July or August.

The autumn foliage of *Quercus borealis*, the red oak, is a coppery-red not unlike that of beech. Rather more subdued but equally lovely autumn colours can be seen on *Fraxinus ornus*, the manna-ash, which turns gold and plum purple.

To set off the red and orange foliage we need some yellow autumn leaves and nothing could be daintier or more elegant than the pale gold foliage of the silver birch. The tall Norway maples also make fine background trees while the shorter field-maple, *Acer campestre*, is usually reluctant to drop its pretty, clear yellow leaves and remains a patch of brightness for weeks.

The leaves of the hornbeams turn to rich gold in autumn and so do their tassels of winged fruits. The liriodendrons, or tulip-trees, wear a similar golden dress and like the hornbeams grow into large and handsome trees. The strange, chopped-off leaves of the liriodendrons are worthy of a close look and the showy green and yellow flowers appearing in midsummer seem suitable for trees that are related to the magnolias.

Hamamelis mollis, the Chinese witch-hazel, is an unbeatable winter-flowering shrub and its yellow autumn leaves are a kind of bonus. The rugosa roses, too, are not considered in the first

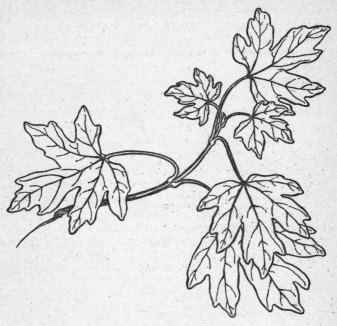

13. *Acer campestre*, the field-maple

place as foliage shrubs but their leaves are often touched with a fine light gold and contrast well with the large red hips.

Ginkgo biloba, the maidenhair-tree, is a deciduous conifer whose foliage has some of the airy daintiness of the silver birch and the whole tree gleams yellow before the leaves begin to fall. On lime-free soil *Taxodium distichum*, the tall and upright swamp cypress, contributes autumn foliage of a warm brownish buttered-toast colour and *Pseudolarix amabilis* (*kaempferi*), the golden larch, looks even more dramatic when its bright green needles turn to richest egg-yolk yellow. The swamp cypress likes a damp spot and will even grow in waterlogged ground, although from my descriptions it might be thought that both these deciduous conifers should be planted in the kitchen garden.

Climbing plants on walls and fences have their share of autumn colours too. Among them, *Parthenocissus quinquefolia* (*Vitis quinquefolia*) is the large-leaved and very strong-growing Virginia creeper whose leaves turn to deepest jewel reds. The even more brilliant *P. tricuspidata* 'Veitchii' (*Ampelopsis veitchii*) is a smaller-leaved creeper which in autumn licks up the sides of buildings like a sheet of flame. The leaves of *P. henryana* (*Vitis henryana*) have pink, white and dark green variegations all summer, in addition to glowing scarlet later in the year, and they show all these colours best on a sunless wall.

Many vines also colour magnificently. *Vitis vinifera* 'Brandt' develops gorgeous red foliage varying from crimson to pink and it carries dark purple grapes. *V. coignetiae* has enormous leaves, in keeping with its strong habit of growth, and in autumn these too are richly coloured.

ORNAMENTAL FRUITS ON TREES AND SHRUBS

Berries dominate the ornamental fruits in our gardens but even if we grow only berrying trees and shrubs their fruits need not all look alike. The berries we can choose vary in size from small beads to large marbles and, apart from numerous red ones, there are yellow, white, black, pink, blue, purple, and lilac berries.

The cotoneasters are a very large group of excellent berrying plants with many other good qualities besides, and with tremendous differences between the species. Some cotoneasters are prostrate shrubs, others are small trees, some are evergreen, some are not, but practically all are handsome, hardy, and easy to grow. Those mentioned in the next paragraph are a few of the most popular evergreen ones with plentiful red berries.

Cotoneaster dammeri is a completely prostrate plant. Its many trailing shoots ooze over the ground and are good weed suppressors. *C. conspicuus decorus* is also used as ground cover but does not grow so flat. It makes a low, dome-shaped bush and its shoots are practically hidden under their load of large round berries. These fruits are not much liked by birds,

14. *Cotoneaster watereri*

so they usually last all winter. *C. franchetii sternianus* and *C. wardii* are two shrubs which resemble one another. Their leaves are green on the upper surface, silvery below, while both plants have very gay orange-red berries. They grow into substantial bushes about six feet tall and the same width. *C. lacteus* makes an even larger bush or a small tree and its leaves, on strong, arching shoots, also have light-coloured undersides. *C. watereri* is a well-known hybrid. Its sturdy trees are quite often planted along roads, where they look very handsome, with profuse, eye-catching berries lasting well into the winter. *C. salicifolius floccosus* is a much smaller, very graceful shrub, with slim leaves and masses of bead-like berries arranged in neat bunches all along its arching stems. *C. exburyensis* and *C. rothschildianus* are two magnificent, strong-growing hybrid cotoneasters, whose large clusters of waxy, light yellow berries remain on the branches for months.

The very spiny berberis, or barberries, are equally beautiful and generous in their fruiting habits, and equally hard to choose between. As with the contoneasters, there are many deciduous and evergreen members of this large genus which will grow well in almost every garden. Most barberries form bushes about six feet tall, although some popular species are smaller, and their yellow flowers are both showy in the mass and individually extremely pretty. I have already mentioned the splendours of several of them in the previous section. The tall, strong-growing evergreen *B. pruinosa* will give an entirely different autumn show. Its deep-green leaves have white undersides and its blue-black berries are covered with white bloom so that they appear pale blue.

The pyracanthas, or fire-thorns, have harder and more leathery-looking berries than the barberries but these too are produced in the greatest profusion and make very fine splashes of colour in the winter garden. Although usually grown against walls, these evergreen cousins of the hawthorns will also make upright bushes in the open border. *Pyracantha coccinea* 'Lalandii' has extra large orange-red berries. *P. watereri* is a hybrid with incredibly heavy crops of bright red berries. *P. crenulata* also has bright red berries and is the best pyracantha for growing on sunless walls. *P. crenulata* 'Flava' (*rogersiana* 'Flava') has most attractive buttercup-yellow berries.

The hawthorns themselves are outstanding berrying trees for exposed gardens. *Crataegus monogyna* and *C. oxycantha*, which are native to this country, have white flowers and deep red berries. There are refined garden forms of both species obtainable with differences in tree shape or flower while one, *C. monogyna* 'Aurea', has bright yellow berries.

A number of varieties of *Sorbus aucuparia*, our native rowan or mountain-ash, are very decorative trees growing well in shallow soil, but the berries ripen and are devoured by birds so early in the year that they make little contribution to the

winter garden. The yellow fruits of *S. a.* 'Xanthocarpa'
('Fructo-luteo') survive longer than the more usual red berries.
S. hupehensis is a Chinese mountain-ash with very large
drooping bunches of berries which are first white, then pale
pink. These fruits last best of all, persisting on the tree for
months.

Botanically speaking, it is only a short step from *Sorbus* to
Malus, the flowering crab-apple. A great many crab-apples
equal the ornamental cherries during their spring show and
surpass them in autumn when their fruits ripen. The trees

15. *Malus* 'Golden Hornet'

usually crop heavily, the cherry-like fruits varying in colour
from yellow flushed with red, through orange, to many true
reds and deep purples. *Malus* 'Golden Hornet' is a magnificent,
upright-growing tree with white flowers and opaque yellow
fruits. *M. purpurea*, a universal favourite, is very well named,
with purplish foliage, clouds of crimson-purple flowers and
crimson fruit also tinged with purple. *M. robusta* is a wonderful sight in autumn and winter. It has quantities of translucent
red fruits weighing down the branches and so bright they seem
to be lit from within. There are, however, so many superb
flowering and fruiting trees in this group that we had best
make a selection after seeing the living plants.

The hollies are almost as difficult as the crab-apples to choose between, not because of much variety in the berries but for the wide range of evergreen foliage they can boast. There is also the fact that male and female flowers are usually carried on separate trees, so if we want both berries and decorative foliage on one tree we must plant the female forms and make sure that there is a male pollinator somewhere nearby. All the named varieties of *Ilex aquifolium*, our native holly, are worth growing. *I. a.* 'Golden King' is really a female and queen of them all for winter brightness, with yellow-margined leaves and bright red berries. 'Argenteo-marginata' is silver-margined and red-berried. 'Bacciflava' ('Fructu-luteo') has green leaves and bright yellow berries, while if we are content with the traditional green foliage and red berries, 'Pyramidalis' is the holly to choose as it is a shapely variety with plenty of fruits and it is also self-fertile.

Holly is always linked in our minds with ivy and *Hedera helix*, the common ivy, it not to be despised as a berrying shrub. Its pale green flowers in autumn are followed by most elegant heads of green-black berries and, although the birds eat them, some usually last until spring.

The viburnums are a large and versatile group of plants enriching the winter garden with flowers, foliage, and berries. Of the fruiting kinds, *Viburnum betulifolium* is supreme, with very numerous bunches of translucent, red-currant-like berries weighing down its bare stems long after the leaves have fallen. *V. opulus*, the guelder-rose, has similar berries. It is a tall shrub or small tree found growing wild in our hedgerows but it can be bought for the garden. There is also a more compact garden form, *V. o.* 'Compactum', and one with yellow berries called 'Xanthocarpum'.

V. tinus, the laurustinus, offers us three kinds of beauty, for not only is it evergreen, but also it blooms all winter and produces berries as well. These are very dark, with a light blue bloom, and, although they are not as showy as the red-currant-like berries, they add to the attractiveness of the bush when they cluster among its leaves and flower heads in late winter. Another viburnum has really conspicuous bright turquoise-

16. *Hedera helix*, the common ivy

blue berries. This is *V. davidii*, a dwarf shrub with handsome, deeply veined evergreen leaves. Both male and female plants must be grown to produce the outstanding berries.

Another shrub with berries in this same rare and beautiful colour is *Clerodendron trichotomum*. This is a fairly large and spreading bush with unremarkable green foliage. Its very sweet-scented white flowers open in late summer and the fruits begin to form soon afterwards. Their colours change from a pale greenish duck-egg blue to the richest turquoise and peacock blues as they ripen. The star-shaped, beetroot-red calices of the flowers persist and frame the berries, making them even more eye-catching.

Symplocos paniculata is sometimes seen giving a brilliant display in large gardens. It is a twiggy shrub or small tree which produces an abundance of bright blue berries when several specimens can pollinate each other, so a good deal of space must be available if the bushes are to fruit successfully.

17. *Clerodendron trichotomum*

For another unusual colour we can grow *Callicarpa bodinieri giraldii* (*Callicarpa giraldiana*). This upright-growing shrub reaches about six feet in height and its pink flowers are followed by clusters of glossy bright lilac berries. These bead-like berries appear most freely when several plants are grouped together and they look enchanting both before and after leaf-fall as the autumn foliage of the callicarpa is tinted with mauve and rose-madder.

In acid soil *Pernettya mucronata* will also provide us with lilac berries and with pink, white, and deep purple-red ones as well. This is a three-foot tall, evergreen shrub with neat foliage and tight clusters of large, hard berries like marbles. To secure the berries little family groups must be grown with a male plant for each three or four females.

Symphoricarpos albus, the snowberry, is a robust strong growing shrub requiring neither special soil conditions nor harem arrangements before producing its opaque white fruits. Snowberries will grow either in the open or under trees and the only complaint their owners are likely to make is that the bushes spread too much by suckers. *S. a. laevigatus* has quantities of pure white 'mothballs' weighing down its branches for a long time after the leaves have gone. *S.* 'Magic Berry' has rosy-mauve fruits while those of 'Mother of Pearl' are waxen pink and white globes, as pretty as they sound.

The names of these two hybrid snowberries bring to mind the pearl berry, *Margyricarpus setosus*. This is a very different shrub, however, being a small prostrate evergreen for the rock garden, with feathery leaves and white berries.

Gaultheria miqueliana is another small evergreen shrub with white or pink berries. It grows about a foot tall and needs a lime-free soil. The red-berried *G. procumbens* is better known and is popular as a ground-covering plant in the same soil. Its smooth oval leaves are bronze tinted in autumn and the plant is known as the partridge-berry.

The pheasant-berry, on the other hand, is one of several common names for *Leycesteria formosa*, a deciduous shrub six feet tall. Its fruits hang in graceful tassels among wine-red-bracts and the glossy berries themselves change from wine-red to black as they ripen. *L. formosa* likes a shady spot and will grow under trees but the bright green of its stems makes a pleasing patch of colour in winter and the plant should not be hidden away out of sight.

The shorter *Mahonia aquifolium* is one of the easiest of shrubs for growing under trees, where it will spread over a wide area. The bloomy blue-black berries have gained the plant its name of Oregon grape. The glossy evergreen foliage is touched with scarlet in winter and *M. aquifolium* can also boast tufts of bright yellow flowers so it is a considerable beauty.

For a more confined space where the rather invasive habits of *Mahonia aquifolium* would not be welcomed, *Skimmia japonica* is a bright and neat evergreen which does well in shade. This is a compact, slow-growing shrub best planted in groups because both male and female forms are needed to produce berries. These large scarlet berries grow in clusters on the female plants and are very nicely set off by glossy leaves. *S. japonica* is a most weather-resistant shrub; the firm, varnished-looking berries last extremely well and in March the bushes are as fresh and attractive as they were the previous November. Added to all these good qualities, both the male and the female flowers smell delicious.

Ruscus aculeatus, the butcher's-broom, is a small evergreen shrub native to this country. It resembles *Skimmia japonica* in several ways, although the two plants could not be confused when we see them side by side. Both thrive in shade and share the same holly-like colours of bright red and glossy dark green but the ruscus has smaller foliage and carries its large marble-sized berries singly, not in clusters.

Botanists tell us that *R. aculeatus* is interesting in that its stiff, sharp-pointed 'leaves' are not leaves at all but flattened stems and it is easy to see that there is something unusual about the plant because each of its tiny flowers rises from the upper surface of one of these 'leaves.'

Another small shrub which berries well in the shade is *Hypericum androsaemum*, the tutsan, also one of our native plants. Its berries sit bolt upright on persistent, starry calices, changing as they ripen from green, through yellow and red, to gleaming black. The shrub is particularly attractive while this is going on and the differently coloured berries look good enough to string on a necklace.

Coming out now from the shade, *Hippophae rhamnoides*, the sea-buckthorn, is a very strong-growing deciduous shrub most at home in open windswept places by the sea. It will also grow inland and is a good shrub for light dry soils. The tall, angular bushes or small trees have slender, silver leaves and in autumn heavy crops of bright orange berries form on female plants if a male pollinator is grown with them. The berries last for months, looking brilliant both against the leaves and afterwards on the bare branches.

Colutea arborescens, the bladder-senna, also does well in

hot dry positions, where it makes a bush about six feet tall.
The neat leaves and the yellow flowers of the bladder-senna
are rather vetch-like and its large inflated pods last into the
winter.

We have left the simple berries behind now and reached
more varied fruits and the spindleberries are among the loveliest
of these, with bright orange seeds emerging from pink or
rose-red capsules. *Euonymus europaeus* is the wild spindle
tree of chalky districts and there are several very showy garden
forms. Among them 'Red Cascade' is outstanding for the

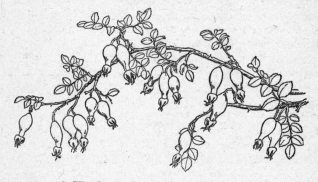

18. The flagon-shaped hips of *Rosa moyesii*

profusion of its fruits and for the richness of their colour, but
to give of its best it needs a wild spindle tree beside it to act
as pollinator. *E. yedoensis* is very similar to *E. europaeus* except
that it grows taller and its fruits hang longer on the branches.

The polished hips of wild roses enliven the country lanes
until birds eat them all and in our gardens some of the shrub
roses make an even brighter show with their conspicuous
fruits. *Rosa moyesii* is famous for its bright red flagon-shaped
hips. These can grow more than two inches long and, being
heavy for the thin flower-stalks, hang by their tails looking
like Martian mice ready to invade. *R. rugosa* 'Frau Dagmar
Hastrup', which gives us clear yellow autumn leaves, has very
large, round, crimson fruits and for a time we can enjoy both

these beauties on the bush along with its last flowers. The grey-foliaged *R. villosa duplex* (*R. pomifera duplex*) is the apple rose, also blessed with the name of Wolley Dod's rose. This is a very bristly shrub, even to its large orange-red fruits, and these resemble gooseberries rather than apples.

Diospyros kaki, the Chinese persimmon, needs hotter summers than we usually experience to ripen its smooth-skinned fruits, but they sometimes colour up well in south-western districts, where they glisten like orange tomatoes among richly tinted autumn leaves.

Growing in sheltered gardens, the fruits of *Cornus capitata* make it look like a carnival edition of the strawberry tree. They swing on longish stems and are a deep rose-pink spotted all over with regularly spaced dark seeds.

Probably the most unusual of all the ornamental fruits we can grow are the deep metallic-blue pods of *Decaisnea fargesii*, which are astonishingly like broad beans in size and shape. This shrub grows up to ten feet high and has pinnate leaves something like the ash.

Chaenomeles, the flowering quince, has golden, apple-like fruits which are rock hard and very long lasting. They look most attractive on the bare branches all winter, and sometimes they are scarcely shrivelled when the bushes begin their next flowering season.

ORNAMENTAL FRUITS ON HERBACEOUS PLANTS

Many herbaceous plants have beautiful seed heads which add interest to the winter garden if they are left to dry on the stems, although we may have to choose either a decorative display of this kind or a longer flowering period from plants which have not been allowed to seed.

Three herbaceous perennials, however, are grown more for their showy fruits than for their flowers. The papery, flame-coloured lanterns of *Physalis franchetii*, the Cape gooseberry, are very well known indeed and are sold by florists in large quantities. *Iris foetidissima*, the stinking iris, has bursting pods of equally bright red seeds. This plant is much more

19. *Decaisnea fargesii*

pleasing than it sounds and has to shoulder an unkind burden
in its name, for only the bruised leaves smell unpleasantly.
Phytolacca clavigera, the pokeberry, is a large leafy plant
growing six feet high and in the autumn tightly packed upright columns of shining black fruits follow its pink flowers.

Chapter Five

Coloured Bark, Tree Shapes, and Foliage Evergreens

In summer we pay little attention to the stems of our plants and we can scarcely be blamed for overlooking them when they are hidden away among flowers and foliage. Once the summer flowers are gone, however, and most of the leaves are down, we begin to appreciate the colours and patterns of tree trunks and bare stems.

BEAUTY IN TREE TRUNKS

Several of the maples whose autumn leaf colour is so brilliant have beautiful trunks as well and provide us with two reasons for including them in the winter garden. *A. palmatum* 'Senkaki' is one of the more shrub-like Japanese maples and it is called the coral-bark maple with good reason as all its young growths are this lovely glowing colour.

Several ornamental cherries rival the maples for winter beauty and *Prunus serrula* is outstanding, with polished coppery-red bark so smooth and gleaming it looks like metal rather than wood.

The black and white trunks of *Betula pendula* (*verrucosa*), the silver birch, are perfect colours for any season and are as satisfying against evergreens in winter as they are among autumn leaves or summer flowers. On the trunk of *Betula papyrifera*, the paper- or canoe-birch, the bark is even whiter than on the silver birch and it is marked all over with small black dashes.

Fraxinus excelsior 'Aurea' is a golden-barked variety of the common ash. It grows into a large tree and looks handsome at all seasons but reaches its peak in autumn when the leaves turn yellow, for then whole branches look as though they were cut out of gold foil.

Pinus sylvestris, the Scots pine, is chiefly planted as a windbreak but it is not without its own rugged beauty and the

20. Decorative tree trunks (left to right) *Pinus sylvestris*, *Prunus serrula*, and *Betula papyrifera*

deeply fissured trunks are very colourful, ranging from reddish-brown to orange and flame in places.

A number of thicket-forming shrubs have brilliantly coloured stems, the dogwoods and the willows being the favourites for ornamental planting. With all these shrubs the young wood is by far the brightest, so bushes grown for winter stem colour are cut hard back almost to ground level each spring.

Among the dogwoods several forms of *Cornus alba* are

available with red stems and *C. a. siberica*, the Westonbirt dogwood, is the most glowing red of all. Two other dogwoods which make a wonderful contrast to this bright red one are *C. baileyi*, with rich red-purple stems, and *C. stolonifera flaviramea*, a subtle greenish-yellow.

The showiest willow is *Salix alba* 'Chermesina', also to be found as *S. vitellina* 'Britzensis'. This plant has orange to vermilion stems and *S. alba* 'Vitellina' practically equals it with a rich chrome-yellow colour. *S. fargesii* has stout stems like polished mahogany set with buds of a brighter red, while *S. daphnoides* is purple with a white bloom.

Some of the bamboos have glaucous green canes and one, *Sinarundinaria nitida*, has dark-purple canes which are very slim and graceful. From the almost black stems of this bamboo we can go to the other end of the colour scale and plant *Rubus cockburnianus*, a tall strong-growing bramble whose stems appear to be white-washed. For a restricted space, *R. thibetanus* is a smaller and less invasive bramble with blue-white stems.

The red-brown stems of many shrub roses look attractive in every gleam of winter sunshine and one, *Rosa omiensis pteracantha*, must be mentioned for the rich wine-red of its translucent thorns.

Bright green stem colour is not very common in winter but we can find it in *Kerria japonica*, the Jew's mallow, and in *Leycesteria formosa*, the pheasant-berry. These two upright shrubs are grown primarily for their flowers and berries, but they make fairly dense clumps of stems which stand out well against either a very dark or a reddish background.

TREE SHAPES

Ornamental bark and coloured stems add beauty to the garden in winter, but when we are considering its all-over design these are details of less importance than the shapes of the plants we choose. The majority of shrubs in the open garden are 'bushy' in shape, that is, they have upright, slightly spreading or branching stems and a more or less rounded outline. For a definite and pleasing contrast to groups of bushy shrubs we can introduce a weeping tree, one with a noticeably twisted habit of growth or one with a slender, tapering silhouette.

Pendulous forms of many well-known trees are obtainable and we can find suitable specimens for any size of garden. Weeping trees should always be given a fairly open position for much of their charm is lost when they are hemmed in by other plants. Among large trees, pendulous forms of the witch-elm, the lime, and of both the green- and the copper-leaved beech are popular for the beauty of their dense, ground-sweeping foliage, but for winter effect I prefer the weeping ash, *Fraxinus excelsior* 'Pendula', with its dramatically down-pointed branches and fanned-out twigs.

The golden-barked weeping willow appears in nursery lists under several names, including *Salix alba* 'Tristis', *S. chryso-coma*, *S.* 'Vitellina Pendula' and *S. babylonica* 'Ramulis Aureis'. This handsome tree looks wonderful in winter when the sun shines on its bare branches but it becomes very large indeed, so the weeping purple willow, *S. purpurea* 'Pendula', is more at home in the average garden. This willow grows little more than twelve feet high.

The common silver birch is a most beautiful tree but, like the weeping willow, too large for many gardens, reaching fifty feet in height. The variety *Betula pendula* 'Youngii', Young's weeping birch, is a smaller tree, between twenty and thirty feet high at maturity, and it is even more pendulous than the silver birch, with the tips of its branches touching the ground.

Among pendulous flowering trees, *Prunus serrulata* 'Rosea', Cheal's weeping cherry, is one of the best known. This small Japanese cherry has a most graceful shape and in late spring the drooping branches are wreathed with double deep pink flowers. *P. subhirtella* 'Pendula' and *P. incisa* 'Moerheimii' are two more pink-flowered weeping cherries while *P. ivensii* has snow-white blossom. *Crataegus monogyna* 'Pendula' is a weeping form of the very hardy common hawthorn, with white flowers, and *C. m.* 'Pendula Rosea' is its pink-flowered sister tree. Two trees with strongly contrasting colours in summer are *Malus* 'Echtermeyer', a crab-apple with bronze foliage and a profusion of purplish-crimson flowers, and *Pyrus salicifolia* 'Pendula', a small pear with silvery-green foliage and cream flowers. The standard form of *Cotoneaster hybridus* 'Pendulus' makes a dainty weeping tree only about eight feet tall. It has clusters of white flowers spaced out along its slender stems and these are followed by bright red berries. *C. h.* 'Pendulus' will not outgrow the smallest garden, and for a number of years I have admired a pair of these little trees growing in two tubs on the pavement outside a town house.

Trees with a twisted habit of growth attract most attention after leaf-fall, when their distinctive skeletons can be plainly seen. *Corylus avellana* 'Contorta', the corkscrew hazel, is well named and looks almost unreal in winter with all its twisted twigs hung with catkins. *Crataegus monogyna* 'Tortuosa', a hawthorn, and *Salix matsudana* 'Tortuosa', a willow, are two more very decorative twisted trees although neither is so extreme in its contortions as the hazel.

Twisted trees must be planted with discretion, because too many would give an uneasy look to the garden, but one will add interest and stand out among more conventional shapes. In much the same way, weeping trees exert a powerful influence on their surroundings and while we usually admire a single specimen or a group planted together, several of them drooping about in different parts of the garden can make it look mournful. Upright trees are not at all depressing, so they can be used both in groups and as single specimens to contrast with lower-growing plants and with the massive shapes of buildings. A spire-like tree also has the advantage of fitting into a small garden better than a tree with a more spreading shape.

The very slim *Prunus* 'Amanogawa', often called the Lombardy poplar cherry, is a favourite deciduous tree for a restricted space. It seldom reaches more than twenty feet in height and its narrow framework of branches is covered with large pale pink flowers in spring. *P. hillieri* 'Spire' is a slightly taller variety, with white blossom. Another flowering tree of moderate size is *Crataegus monogyna* 'Stricta', an erect-growing white-flowered hawthorn. *Liriodendron tulipifera* 'Fastigiata' is a distinguished upright form of the tulip-tree

21. Slender trees: Lombardy poplar, Dawyck beech, incense cedar, and (in front) *Prunus* 'Amanogawa'

and larger than the other flowering trees mentioned here.

The Lombardy poplar, *Populus nigra* 'Italica', is a magnificent columnar tree which can grow to a height of one hundred feet in about thirty years. With it tremendous height and wide root spread it is, of course, only suitable for the largest of gardens and for a position where it can dominate the landscape. But in spite of its impressive turn of speed the Lombardy poplar is not our fastest-growing tall tree. I have been reading about a hybrid poplar, *Populus* 'Androscoggin', which is breaking all records and must be related to Jack's Beanstalk. It is reported to reach a height of one hundred feet in only fifteen years.

Leaving the giants in a class by themselves, *Betula pendula* 'Fastigiata', an upright form of the silver birch, can be found a place in a moderately sized garden for, although it may eventually reach fifty to sixty feet, it grows slowly without robbing the soil unduly and is always an elegant tree.

Quercus robur 'Fastigiata', an erect form of the common oak, makes a massive cone-shaped tree for a large garden and another tree for a spacious setting is the taller and more slender Dawyck beech, *Fagus sylvatica* 'Fastigiata'. Both these trees have handsome foliage and rich autumn leaf colour. For a rather less solid-looking tree with clear yellow autumn leaves we could choose *Ginkgo biloba* 'Fastigiata', an upright form of the maidenhair-tree, which is a deciduous conifer.

The conifers also provide almost all our slender evergreen trees. They vary greatly in the colour of their foliage and among those forming slim columns are trees of all sizes from rock garden miniatures to forest giants, so no one should have difficulty in finding suitable evergreen 'exclamation marks' among the conifers to punctuate the winter garden display.

Juniperus communis 'Compressa' is a tiny greyish-green spire which seldom outgrows a place on the rockery because it creeps up so very slowly and reaches only three feet at maturity. For general garden planting several varieties of Lawson cypress make quite small columnar trees. Among them, *Chamaecyparis lawsoniana* 'Elwoodii' is popular for its blue-grey foliage and its modest height of eight to nine feet. *C.l.* 'Columnaris' is a taller blue-grey tree reaching more than twenty feet in height and its very narrow outline makes it resemble the Italian cypress, which is so well known round the Mediterranean coasts. In this country, *Cupressus sempervirens* 'Stricta', the slender Italian cypress itself, needs a good deal of protection when it is young but it is a strikingly beautiful tree. *Cupressus arizonica* is a hardier tree of much the same shape, with blue-grey foliage.

Taxus baccata 'Fastigiata', the Irish yew, is a stout, very dark green conifer reaching twenty feet and more in height but its variety *T. b.* 'Fastigiata Standishii' is much smaller in all its dimensions and very slow growing. It makes a slim column of dense golden-yellow foliage about six feet tall.

Now that *Cupressocyparis leylandii*, the Leyland cypress, is easy to obtain it is being widely planted in screening belts but an isolated specimen makes a most symmetrical grey-green cone-shaped tree for a large garden and it grows quickly to its full height of about fifty feet. Tallest and slimmest of all for ornamental plantings is the incense-cedar, *Libocedrus decurrens*, a superb tree with dark green foliage. It is capable of reaching seventy feet or more in height while retaining the shape of a giant pencil.

Apart from slender trees like those mentioned above there are a great many beautiful conifers with wider based, more pyramidal outlines and these too make impressive features among lower and more rounded forms.

FOLIAGE EVERGREENS

All the evergreen conifers in the last section are, of course, grown for their foliage effect as well as for their shape and a list of all the conifers with fine winter foliage would be very long indeed. It would certainly have to include some more varieties of the versatile Lawson cypress, particularly *Chamaecyparis lawsoniana* 'Erecta', a bright green pyramidal tree, *C. l.* 'Albo-spica', with its green foliage variegated with white so that it looks paint splashed, *C. l.* 'Lutea', with very bright, almost canary-yellow foliage, and *C. l.* 'Minima', a grey-green bee-hive of a plant.

Among other attractive conifers not already mentioned, *Abies arizonica* 'Compacta' is a neat little silver fir and *Picea pungens* 'Glauca' is like a blue-frosted Christmas tree. There are several particularly good blue forms of this Colorado spruce so it is best to see the plants which are being offered before placing an order. *P. omorika* 'Pendula', the weeping Serbian spruce, is a graceful, quick-growing tree whose down-flowing branches are covered with dark green and silver needles.

Cryptomeria japonica 'Elegans' is a tall, bushy conifer with feathery light green foliage in summer and most striking winter foliage of rich coppery-red. *Thuya occidentalis* 'Rheingold' is a less tall but very broad tree which also changes its coat according to the season. Its summer foliage is a light gold and in winter this becomes rich bracken-gold and bronze.

Juniperus sabina tamariscifolia is quite different from the dapper upright *J. communis* 'Compressa' but both plants are at home on a rockery. *J. s. tamariscifolia* is a low-spreading conifer which flows in a green waterfall over uneven ground and looks very picturesque among rocks, while on a level site it assumes the perfectly circular flattened shape of a millstone.

Next to the conifers, the hollies are probably the trees most widely planted for winter colour and several good berrying forms have been included among ornamental fruiting trees in Chapter Four. *Ilex aquifolium* 'Golden Queen' and *I. a.* 'Silver Queen' are misleadingly named male trees, one with yellow- and one with white-margined leaves. Both are beautifully glossy hollies and so is another unfortunate male tree, *I. a.* 'Golden Milkmaid', whose handsome yellow leaves are edged with green. The hedgehog holly, *I. a.* 'Ferox', is another male plant and we cannot cavil at this name because its abundant spines rise from the surface of the leaves as well as from their edges and the tree is a very prickly customer indeed.

Elaeagnus pungens 'Maculata' 'Aurea Variegata' looks at first glance like another holly. It is the brightest of all our gold and green variegated shrubs. Most of its shining leaves have dark green margins and are boldly splashed with canary yellow, while occasional leaves are practically all yellow. The thin stems are a warm reddish-brown and the whole bush makes an unbeatable patch of winter colour.

Aucuba japonica 'Variegata', the variegated Japanese laurel, is a very well-known shrub often used for hedges, but it is handsome enough to be grown as a single specimen which will show off the splashes and speckles of bright yellow on its polished leaves. Two more easily grown and glossy evergreens are *Prunus laurocerasus*, the common laurel, and *P. lusitanica*,

22. *Elaeagnus pungens* 'Maculata'

the Portugal laurel. *Lauris nobilis*, the bay tree, is a large shrub with shapely aromatic leaves.

Among small-leaved evergreens, we can find many bushy shrubs with either plain green or variegated foliage. *Buxus sempervirens* is the common box growing wild on the chalk hills and several very attractive, gold-variegated garden forms of this box are obtainable. *Ligustrum ovalifolium* is the privet which could no doubt girdle the Earth if all the hedges grown from it were placed end to end, but although taken so much for granted its variegated forms are pretty shrubs. *Ligustrum ovalifolium* 'Aureo-marginatum' is the golden privet with green-centred yellow leaves, while *L. o.* 'Argenteum' is very similar, with creamy-white variegations. *Euonymus japonica* is another hedge-making shrub with exceedingly shiny green leaves and there are a number of forms with gold- and silver-variegated foliage.

In mild districts with acid soil *Eucalyptus gunnii* is a charming sight in winter. The trees have two kinds of foliage, round blue-green 'pennies' on young specimens and longer sickle-shaped leaves on mature trees. The dainty evergreen *Pittosporum tenuifolium* also needs a mild climate. This shrub has a great many small waxy pale green leaves on very thin black stems.

Choisya ternata, the Mexican orange-blossom, is a first-class flowering shrub with flat heads of very lovely white flowers in May, but its distinctive three-lobed leaves and dense bushy habit of growth earn it an honoured place as a foliage evergreen as well.

Trees and large shrubs are not, however, the only evergreens to beautify the winter garden. Ivies will clothe fences and tree stumps, or they will act as ground cover along with many other low-growing and trailing evergreen plants. *Hedera helix* is our very tough and hardy wild ivy and there are many named varieties of it with either green or variegated foliage, and some have most intriguing leaf shapes.

To pick out just a few, *Hedera helix* 'Cristata' has pale green frilly leaves, 'Sagittaefolia' is darker green, with pointed, arrow-shaped leaves, 'Buttercup' is a bright yellow, and 'Marginata' ('Silver Queen') has green white-margined leaves tinged with pink in winter. *H. chrysocarpa*, the Italian ivy, has very bright green leaves, some of which are suffused with coppery-red in winter. *H. colchica*, the Persian ivy, is a very large-leaved and tall-growing climber. This ivy will quickly cover a wall with its six- to nine-inch leaves of glossy dark green, and *H. c.* 'Variegata' is its even more handsome variety with pale yellow and green foliage.

Heathers and heaths thrive in acid soil, where they are valued as much for their evergreen foliage as for their flowers. In Chapter Three I have mentioned some varieties of the common heather, *Calluna vulgaris* and some brightly coloured varieties of it are available among a larger number with deep green foliage. *C. v.* 'Aurea' has golden foliage tipped with red and orange in winter, while the young shoots of 'Argentea' are silvery white. 'Hirsuta' has grey felty-looking foliage, 'Searlei Aurea' has mid-green foliage, lime-yellow at the tips, and 'Ruth Sparkes' has vivid lime-green to yellow foliage. *Erica tetralix* 'Mollis' is a cross-leaved heath with light grey-green foliage and the golden foliage of *E. cinerea* 'Golden Drop' turns to copper and rosy-red in winter.

Coming to other carpeting evergreens, *Arctostaphylos uva-ursi*, despite its resounding name, is no more than the small green-leaved bear-berry which creeps about on our northern moors. It needs lime-free soil and a sunny position to do well. *Vaccinium vitis-idaea* is the slightly larger but similar cow-berry, another pretty little evergreen for open heathy places.

Galax aphylla is a carpeting evergreen from the woods of Virginia and Alabama. It has quite large shining leaves and small spikes of white flowers resembling those of our native wintergreen. Like the bear-berry, it prefers lime-free soil but it grows and spreads in the shade of trees. *Pachysandra terminalis* is a low-growing Japanese evergreen shrub for the same position. It also has spikes of white flowers and these appear very early in the year.

Hypericum calycinum, the rose-of-Sharon, is a better-known carpeting plant which thrives in poor soil and in dense shade. It is a strong-growing and invasive plant, as it has to be to overcome such difficult growing conditions, but, apart from its utility as a foliage ground cover, its wide-open, golden-yellow flowers in summer are very beautiful.

The periwinkles, *Vinca major* and *V. minor*, also spread widely but much is forgiven them for growing and blooming in sun or shade and covering bare ground under trees with their neat and attractive foliage. There are variegated forms of both these periwinkles and the named varieties of *V. minor* have bright-eyed starry flowers in spring, ranging from white through blue and mauve to deep purple.

Like the periwinkles, the variegated dead-nettles are exceedingly decorative and easy to please. Both *Lamium maculatum* and *L. galeobdolon* 'Variegatum' (*Galeobdolon luteum* 'Variegatum') grow strongly in sun or shade and, planted under trees, they light up the ground in winter with a dappled carpet of green and silver leaves, but are very invasive.

SILVER-LEAVED EVERGREENS

Most of the green-leaved and variegated evergreens will grow and look well in either sun or partial shade, but the silver-leaved plants, although they may survive, lose all their gleaming beauty and fade to dull green in a badly lit position. They also prefer a light, well-drained soil, so both these facts must be kept in mind when we decide to use silver evergreens to brighten the winter garden.

Rosemary and lavender, two aromatic cottage-garden favourites, make a good foundation for a collection of silver evergreens. *Rosmarinus officinalis* is the common rosemary, which forms a bush up to seven feet tall and is an excellent background shrub for smaller and more brightly coloured plants. *Lavendula spica*, the old English lavender, is usually much lower-growing than rosemary, only three feet high or less. *Teucrium fruticans* is another blue-flowered shrub related to rosemary and lavender. All three of these shrubs are silver-grey rather than silver and so is the reliable *Senecio laxifolius* which grows into a three-foot bush and thrives in heavier soils than most of the plants in this section. The much showier *S. cineraria* 'Ramparts' is a bright-looking plant with segmented, white-felted leaves. It makes a shapely rounded bush but is not completely hardy. 'White Diamond' is a very similar variety with leaves of an even more sparkling silver. *S. leucostachys* is a thin-stemmed lacy shrub with very elegant and finely cut foliage. It needs the protection of a warm wall. *Artemisia arborescens* is another dainty silver-foliaged shrub for the same position; it will support itself quite well in a sheltered border.

The santolinas, or lavender-cottons, are hardier than the last few plants mentioned and both *S. chamaecyparissus* and *S. neapolitana* make neat hummocks of finely cut silver-grey foliage.

A number of shrubby helichrysums have bright silver foliage and the hardiest of these is *Helichrysum splendidum* (*H. alveolatum*) which grows between two and three feet tall. *H. plicatum* is another attractive, slightly smaller-growing species for a warm sheltered position.

Atriplex halimus, the tree-purslane, is a semi-evergreen with arching branches clothed in silver-grey leaves. It can grow into a large bush up to eight feet tall and, like most of its family, does particularly well at the seaside. A number of its less aristocratic relations camp out on our seashores.

23. Grey-leaved evergreens, three senecios

To complete this section here are two plants whose foliage goes rather well with the pure silvers. *Phlomis fruticosa*, the Jerusalem sage, has grey-green woolly leaves set in pairs all up its stems and makes a bushy shrub about three feet tall. *Ruta graveolens* 'Jackman's Blue' is a rue with lacy foliage of a particularly fine blue-grey and this plant grows into a neat bush somewhat smaller than the Jerusalem sage.

Chapter Six

Winter Flowers

Most of the plants mentioned here are hardy but their flowers may be damaged by frost, wind, or driving rain, so there is always an element of luck in whether or not we enjoy a successful display during bad winters. To lessen the odds against them, winter-blooming plants should be given favourable positions in the garden. Plants grown on walls and fences and those sheltered by buildings or on the lee side of tough shrubs stand the best chance of opening unblemished flowers. Most plants enjoy winter sunshine, even those which need shade later on, but, because the morning sun shining on frosted flowers can cause severe damage, a position open to the east should not be chosen for winter-blooming plants.

Birds, too, can do a lot of damage by pecking out flower buds and when they are known to be troublesome it is a help to string black cotton over plants before the buds begin to colour. Solitary flowering plants suffer more from birds than large groups of the same plant. This is partly because damage to a single specimen is more noticeable, of course, but also because birds tend to go for the 'odd-man-out' among garden plants just as they will attack one of themselves who is different from the rest.

I have also noticed that new plants are sometimes damaged the first time they bloom but left alone in following years, as though everything growing in their territory had either to be taught a lesson by the resident birds or else tried for flavour before being marked 'Tested. Edible in emergencies'.

Slugs unfortunately are less selective and all we can do about them is to keep the numbers down as far as possible.

SHRUBS

Daphne mezereum 'Grandiflora', the last plant mentioned in the chapter on autumn flowers, can be taken as the first of the winter-blooming shrubs because it continues to open its reddish-purple flowers at intervals until February.

After using the daphne as a link with the autumn flowers I must lose no more time before introducing the hardest working shrub of the winter garden, *Prunus subhirtella* 'Autumnalis', the autumn cherry. The common name does not do justice

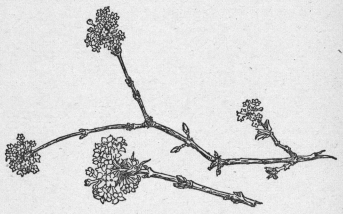

24. *Viburnum fragrans*

to this prunus, because it begins to bloom in November and from then until the end of March the pink buds open inter- mittently into little showers of fragile white cherry blossom during any spell of reasonable weather. The autumn cherry can be grown either as a bush or as a standard tree which eventually reaches twenty to twenty-five feet.

Two viburnums can be relied upon to bloom all winter. First the evergreen *Viburnum tinus*, the laurustinus, mentioned in Chapter Four. *Viburnum fragrans* is a deciduous shrub with clustered white or pink-tinged flower heads at the ends of its stems and on its many short stiff side growths. *V. bodnan-tense* 'Dawn' is a very fine hybrid viburnum closely resembling *V. fragrans* but with more numerous and larger flowers in a particularly lovely rosy-pink. *V. bodnantense* 'Deben' is another beauty, growing rather taller. All these deciduous viburnums have a sweet, nutty scent that reminds me of marzipan. Like the autumn cherry, they go on opening their flowers in succession until early spring.

Jasminum nudiflorum, the winter jasmine, is one of the finest and also one of the easiest winter-blooming shrubs flowering over a long period. The red-splashed yellow buds and clear yellow flowers, which begin to appear in November, continue to clothe its green shoots for the next five months. It flourishes in all soils, in town or country and in sun or shade. All the young growth is thin and floppy so *J. nudiflorum* needs some support. It is usually grown against walls or over arbours and if only the main stems are tied in the younger growth makes an arching, flowery cascade. Used as ground cover it will flow over a sloping bank and root at the tips of the branches to form new plants.

Going now from cottage to castle, the aristocratic evergreen camellias are not so easily accommodated because they will grow only in lime-free soils and some need a lot of protection. Contrary to a widely held belief, however, many camellias are quite hardy although their flowers can be spoilt by frost. Among the winter-blooming camellias, varieties of the hybrid *C. williamsii* are very popular and their colours include the most delicate of shell-pinks. One of them, 'November Pink', will flower for a very long time in a sheltered position, opening its first blooms in November and continuing until spring. *C. sasanqua* and its varieties also contribute many beautiful rose-like flowers to the winter show but except in mild districts the plants need the protection of a wall. *C. s.* 'Narumi-Gata' has pure white petals round a boss of golden stamens and it begins to bloom in November. *C. japonica* is a completely hardy plant and there are innumerable varieties of it carrying white, pink, or rich red flowers and blooming from late winter until late spring.

The callunas and ericas, too, are easier for those who garden on acid soil, but, fortunately for the rest of us, all the varieties of *Erica carnea* can tolerate lime. Planted closely together the evergreen foliage of callunas and ericas creates a cosy winter carpet of greys and greens shot with gold, clear yellow, copper, and red, while the fact that it need never be without flowers makes this kind of patchwork planting doubly attractive.

Although most often thought of as autumn-flowering plants,

25. Camellia japonica

several varieties of *Calluna vulgaris*, the common heather, bloom in early winter. These need an acid soil and they include *C. v.* 'Searlei', a very fine white, *C. v. hibernica*, pinkish-mauve, and *C. v.* 'David Eason', deep red-purple. Also in bloom before Christmas is the neat white heath, *Erica carnea* 'Snow Queen', and the equally compact *E. c.* 'King George' with deep pink flowers. These ericas continue to bloom for about two months and before they are finished the vigorous *E. c.* 'Springwood White' and *E. c.* 'Springwood Pink' take over. The Springwoods are very spreading, free blooming plants about six inches high.

A contrast in both shape and colour is provided by *E. darleyensis*, an upright, lime-tolerant heath which grows eighteen inches to two feet tall and blooms from November until late March. It has mauve-pink flowers. Beginning to bloom in March and continuing until early summer are all the varieties of *E. mediterranea*, tall heaths which are lime-tolerant and can be introduced very successfully into the heather garden not only for their later flowers but to give variety of shape among the low ground-hugging kinds.

Leaving these carpeting plants now and turning to an evergreen climber for growing on walls, the small bell flowers of *Clematis balearica* come and go all winter. They are not very striking from a distance but on closer examination they are seen to be a very pretty subdued yellow speckled with red. The ferny, bronze-tinted foliage of this climber is its most obvious attraction but altogether it is a very dainty and attractive plant.

The flowers of *Chimonanthus praecox*, the winter-sweet, have the same failing as the flowers of this clematis and look a rather muddy fawn from the distance but here too a closer look reveals their beauty. The basic colour of the flowers is pale yellow and the inner petals are delicately pencilled with reddish-purple. They open on the bare twigs from December onwards and have one of the most delicious scents imaginable. Added to the scent of the flowers, *C. praecox* can boast another kind of fragrance for it is an aromatic shrub related to the allspice, a North American plant. The cut ends of twigs, or any part of its wood which is crushed, have a pleasant spicy smell. Although it is not tender, *C. praecox* grows best and blooms most freely against a warm wall. It does not bloom for the first few years of its life, but is worth waiting for.

Hamamelis mollis, the Chinese witch-hazel, is another star performer in the winter garden. It begins to bloom several weeks before Christmas and continues for about three months. The odd spidery flowers have very narrow bright yellow petals and they grow in clusters all over the bare twigs where they open continuously in all but the most severe frosty weather. Even this does not harm the flowers, they simply wait curled up until the temperature rises a little and then go on blooming as gaily as before. *H. m.* 'Pallida' has paler, almost lemon-yellow flowers and there are other varieties obtainable, some with reddish flowers, but these are not nearly so striking as the yellows. The witch-hazel prefers acid soil but will settle down in a limy soil to which peat has been added. When I grew it in these circumstances the shrub bloomed very well indeed and only the colour of its autumn leaves suffered.

A green-flowered shrub which blooms at this time is *Fatsia japonica*. Better known perhaps as a house plant, this tropical-looking evergreen is quite hardy and thrives in seaside gardens. I have seen it growing and flowering well on the Suffolk coast, which is not famed for its balmy climate. The glossy palmate leaves of *F. japonica* are very large and the lighter green flowers grow in spherical heads held well up above the foliage on stiff branching stalks.

In December the shrubby honeysuckle, *Lonicera fragrantissima*, usually begins to bloom and it continues until March. It is a semi-evergreen plant which grows into a large bush. Its chief attraction is in the sweet scent rather than the appearance of its creamy-yellow flowers. These are pretty enough, but they are rather small and stubby, not quite the kind of flower the name honeysuckle conjures up. *L. purpusii* is a larger-flowered hybrid honeysuckle with *L. fragrantissima* as one of its parents. It has inherited the sweet scent and also blooms in winter.

Another exceedingly fragrant shrub is the evergreen *Azara microphylla* which opens its diminutive vanilla-scented flowers in February, but needs the protection of a sunny wall.

About this time, although we are still in the middle of winter, the longer days begin to make themselves felt and a number of shrubs come into bloom in February. *Daphne mezereum* and its white counterpart 'Alba' join *D. m.* 'Grandiflora', which has been showing them what to do all winter. Two evergreen daphnes also begin to bloom, the deliciously scented *D. odora*, with small clusters of mauve flowers at the ends of its twigs, and *D. laureola*, with hanging bunches of small yellow-green flowers below the leaves. *D. laureola* is the spurge-laurel, which is found growing wild under trees in chalky districts and it can be used for the same purpose in gardens. *D. odora* is one of our most outstanding scented plants and deserves a place in any collection of shrubs. It is usually grown against a wall in cold districts and it blooms at intervals for months. There is a form with gold-edged leaves which is said to be hardier than the plain green-foliaged plant.

Mahonia japonica is another contender for the title of 'Miss Fragrance'. This evergreen shrub likes to open a few tentative

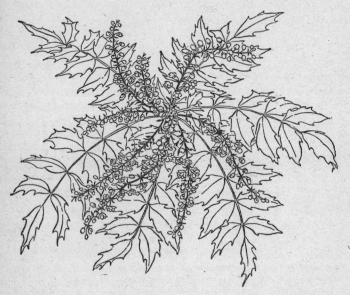

26. *Mahonia japonica*

flowers at odd times all winter but by February it is in full bloom and its arching sprays of small primrose-yellow flowers are scenting the air all round it. The foliage is very handsome too, the glossy dark green segmented leaves acting as a foil for the flowers which grow in terminal clusters.

The only real difficulty in the culture of this shrub is in obtaining the true *M. japonica*. Nurserymen are apt to supply its relative *M. bealei* under this name and although quite a fine plant *M. bealei* has only a stumpy, upright tuft of flowers, so we had best see the plants which are being offered in bloom before ordering them. *M.* 'Charity' is a striking-looking hybrid very similar to *M. japonica.* Its flowers are more densely clustered on their graceful stems, but when I have been able to compare the two shrubs I have thought it much less fragrant than *M. japonica.*

Cornus mas, the Cornelian cherry, has bright yellow flowers of quite a different kind. They grow in much the same way as the flowers of *Viburnum fragrans,* clustered at the ends of every twig, and in February the bushes look delightful when they are bare of leaves but dotted all over with pom-poms of fully opened flowers.

As a background for the gay flowers of *Cornus mas,* nothing could be better than the quiet colours of *Garrya elliptica* growing against a wall. This tall, dense evergreen has dull, medium-green leaves and is thickly hung with paler grey-green catkins. These form early in the winter, hanging in tassels and gradually lengthening until in February or March, having reached their full size, they open fluffy bands of cream-coloured stamens. There are both male and female forms of *G. elliptica* but the male catkins are the more spectacular.

At the other end of the scale from the tall garrya, *Ribes laurifolium* is a green-flowered dwarf shrub blooming in February and March. It has dark, glossy, evergreen foliage and hanging bunches of very light green flowers similar in shape to those of its well-known cousins the flowering currants.

Sarcococca humilis is another dwarf evergreen flowering at this time. It has small stiff leaves and the very fragrant little white flowers dangle close to its stems. *S. humilis* grows about twelve inches high. It is not at all striking to look at but it makes a useful ground cover under taller shrubs, the scent of the flowers is very sweet, and in autumn it carries glossy black berries.

For really brilliant flowers in late winter nothing could be prettier than the deciduous *Rhododendron mucronulatum,* which carries its small, bright, rosy-purple flowers on the tips of bare shoots in late January and February. *R. praecox,* a semi-evergreen hybrid rhododendron, follows *R. mucronula-tum* and can smother itself completely with light mauve blooms in February and March. These shrubs, like all rhododendrons, need acid soil and, although the plants are hardy, the delicate flowers can be spoilt by frost.

Rhododendrons are out of the question for gardens on limy ground but the early flowering prunus have no objection to lime and will supply these gardens with gay colour in February. *Prunus conradinae* is a small cherry-tree whose white or faintly pink blossom begins to appear in February and takes over the scene as *P. subhirtella autumnalis* is reaching the end of its long flowering period. *P. incisa* 'February Pink' is another early-flowering cherry, which usually grows in bush form and whose flowers live up to their name. *P. mume*, the Japanese apricot, also blooms in February and *P. m.* 'Brightness' is particularly charming with deep pink flowers set off by fluffy white stamens. *P. davidiana* 'Alba', a Chinese peach with pure white flowers starring the bare stems, is a beautiful companion for 'Brightness'. The very well-known almonds bloom early in the year too; *P. amygdalus* is the common almond, which makes a strong tree and has clusters of pale pink single flowers. White and double-flowered varieties can also be found.

Abeliophyllum distichum is a relative of the forsythia and looks extremely like its popular cousin. The abeliophyllum is not so robust or strong growing as forsythia, but it is a very dainty shrub with quantities of sweet-scented flowers appearing in February and March. *A. distichum* is usually described in catalogues as having pink buds opening white, but the few bushes I have seen had flowers which were more pink than white. The general impression is of a pink shrub and it is very attractive indeed against a grey wall.

The forsythias themselves herald the spring in rows of suburban gardens and are none the worse for being so easy and vigorous, although the crude yellows of some varieties do unkind things to the pale pink almonds so often grown beside them. *F. giraldiana* is a very early-flowering species which has graceful sprays of pale yellow flowers and against a warm

wall these can open in January. *F. ovata* is another early
species which follows closely on the heels of the first. There
are now so many forsythias obtainable that it is best to see the
plants in bloom before ordering them. One person's idea of an
attractive yellow may not agree with another's, and, as the
flowers come before the leaves, it is their colour, size, and
spacing which makes all the difference to the appearance of
these handsome and reliable shrubs.

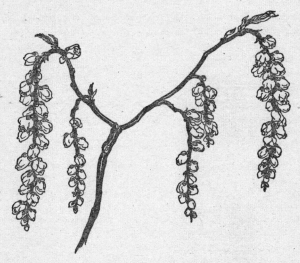

27. *Stachyurus praecox*

Stachyurus praecox is a much less flamboyant yellow-
flowered shrub than forsythia but a very beautiful one. Its
flower buds form in autumn and hang all winter on the naked
branches like strings of green beads. In February the strings
lengthen and the buds swell into waxy, primrose-yellow
flowers. Not many nurseries stock this plant, but bushes of
both this species and of the very similar *S. chinensis* can be
seen in Kew Gardens, mostly in mixed shrub borders under
deciduous trees. As it is slightly tender, stachyurus appreciates
this kind of shelter and it will also grow well against a wall.

Corylopsis is another bushy shrub with drooping yellow flowers. It blooms at the same time or a little later than *Stachyurus praecox* and, unlike it, is quite easy to obtain. Its cowslip-shaped flowers hang from the bare twigs in tight bunches which lengthen into tassels as they open. In some species the flowers are prettily frilled with stamens and most are sweet scented. *C. pauciflora* is a dwarf shrub growing three to four feet tall. *C. spicata*, which grows taller, reaching six feet, also has longer tassels of flowers.

Turning from yellow to white flowers, *Pieris japonica*, is an outstanding evergreen shrub for acid soils. The foliage is a glossy, dark green and in late February or March the brown furry-looking spikes of flower buds, which have been waiting at the ends of twigs since the previous autumn, open into cascades of waxy white bells like lilies-of-the-valley. *P. japonica* grows into a large bush, eventually reaching ten feet in height, and there are several other species of pieris in cultivation, all with similar flowers.

Magnolia stellata is the smallest magnolia grown in our gardens. It flowers when very young and begins to bloom each year in late February or March. The many-petalled flowers are pure white and open from slender, felt-covered buds to the large flat stars which give the plant its name. After reaching their full spread the petals droop and hang raggedly, but this scarcely affects the beauty of the bush and fresh young flowers opening in succession distract our attention from those fading. Several other magnolias bloom at the same time of year, but these are all tall trees which grow for many seasons before they even think about flowering.

The furry catkins of the 'pussy-willows' are in a different class from the flowers of magnolias, but they are delightful in their own way. The male and female catkins of all willows are carried on separate plants and it is the pollen-covered male flowers which turn yellow, so if golden pussy-willows are wanted male plants must be grown. *Salix caprea*, the great sallow, is our large native pussy-willow which grows into a tree twenty feet or more high and flowers in March and April. *S. medemii*, a small shrubby willow, is more suitable for the

28. *Magnolia stellata*

garden. It blooms early, in February or March, and is very decorative when the fat silver-grey catkins turn yellow.

Red flowered shrubs for the winter garden are not common. *Parrotia persica*, a hardy deciduous tree or tall bush belonging to the witch-hazel family, is one of the few. Early in the year it produces attractive, small, red flowers clustering close to its

bare stems. The flowers are sometimes described as being
scarlet but to me they look a rather more subdued red.

For really bright reds we must depend on chaenomeles, the
flowering quince, still known to most gardeners as 'Cydonia' or
'Japonica'. There are several species and many fine varieties of
this shrub to provide blooms from early March until June. All
have flowers resembling apple blossom and they can be
obtained in any red or flame colour we like to think of. Apart
from the reds, there are chaenomeles with beautiful pink or
pure white flowers. The shrubs are not at all tender but when
they are trained against walls or fences they usually begin to
bloom earlier than they do in the open border.

HERBACEOUS PLANTS

One reason for the popularity of *Helleborus niger*, the Christmas-rose, is that it begins to bloom in early winter, a distinction
shared by very few herbaceous plants in our gardens. The
snowy-white flowers of *H. niger* are so beautiful, conspicuous,
and long-lasting that they could scarcely be overlooked even
in midsummer. They are carried above evergreen foliage and
the plant is completely hardy, but, because the flowers are
often only a few inches from the ground, they can be damaged
by slugs and splashed with mud. *H. niger* 'Potter's Wheel' is a
fine variety of Christmas-rose with broad, overlapping petals
and very large flowers. *H. niger* is not, however, the only evergreen hellebore to grace the winter garden. *H. orientalis* is
the Lenten-rose, with flowers ranging from white stained with
pink and green, through purplish-pinks to deep plum-purple.
In some forms the pale flowers are prettily stippled with a
darker colour. This is a larger plant than *H. niger* and has
stems about fifteen inches high. Although many varieties of
H. orientalis bloom from January until April, some begin before
Christmas. *H. o. atrorubens*, with rich red-purple flowers, is
one of the earliest to bloom. *H. corsicus* (*argutifolius*) is a larger
plant still, making stout clumps of evergreen, tooth-edged
leaves eighteen inches to two feet high. The nodding flowers
are borne in large clusters and when a number of them are

29. *Helleborus niger*, the 'Christmas-rose'

open in January or February *H. corsicus* is a symphony in green, with dark, grey-green foliage and with conspicuous yellow-green stamens in the pale apple-green flowers. This hellebore also begins to bloom before Christmas in some seasons.

Vinca diformis, one of the periwinkles, is less striking than the hellebores and not quite so hardy, but it is a notable plant for the winter garden as it also blooms in November and December. It is a low-growing scrambling evergreen with glossy leaves set neatly in pairs. Its pale-mauve, starry flowers

T–D

are halfpenny-sized and cluster on short stems, while longer
barren stems sprawl over the ground. The very hardy *V. major*
and *V. minor*, the greater and lesser periwinkles, both open
occasional flowers in midwinter, but their main flowering
season does not begin before March.

Viola tricolor is one of the parents of the well-loved pansy of
our summer gardens. Specially bred hybrid pansies can be
grown for winter flowers and they are gay little plants but,
although perennial, they are not very long lived. When they
are used for formal bedding or when any really important
patch of colour is planned young plants are set out each year
in late summer. These plants begin to bloom in autumn and
their flowers open at intervals all winter during mild spells,
continuing until late spring. In midwinter the yellow varieties
show up best and seem to be less battered by the weather than
those with violet blooms.

Parochetus communis, the shamrock-pea, is well described
by its common name. It is a trailing plant, making mats of
clover-like foliage and adorned with pure blue pea-flowers. The
flowers are large compared with the size of the plant, they are
carried just clear of the foliage and appear over a long season.
P. communis is not entirely hardy and is sometimes grown as a
greenhouse plant, but in a sheltered spot out of doors its
lovely flowers will keep on appearing from November until
spring.

Iris unguicularis (*stylosa*) needs a warm, sunny, well-drained
spot and is usually seen blooming well at the base of a south-
facing wall. The exquisite flowers are a very delicate, pale
lilac with darker pencillings and most of them appear in
January and February from rather untidy tufts of long,
grass-like foliage. The blooms of this iris are just as fragile as
they look and in bad weather they are quickly spoilt, but the
buds open well in water so we can always make sure of a
few perfect flowers indoors when the garden is being swept
with wind and rain.

The close relations of *Primula vulgaris*, our common primrose, are early astir and the wild flower itself can be found
opening mild eyes in sheltered nooks all through the winter.

30. *Primula denticulata*, the drumstick primula, and a Juliana hybrid
primula

Invited into the garden their pale, slightly greenish-yellow is
one of the prettiest foils for the blue-flowered cultivated
primroses. *P. juliae*, a more dwarf plant than *P. vulgaris*, has
deep wine-red flowers in winter and early spring. It is one
parent of the many lovely early-flowering primroses which are
known collectively as 'Juliana hybrids' and cover a wide range
of colours including blues, mauves, pinks and purples. *P.*
'Wanda' is one of these, with magenta-crimson flowers and

is rather looked down upon by some gardeners because of its crude colour, but it is a generous little plant and can be relied upon for a few blooms at odd times long before its main display in February and March. *P. denticulata*, growing a foot tall, is commonly called the drumstick primula and this is a good name for the plant, with its globular heads of tightly packed flowers on straight stalks. Beginning to bloom in late February, it is easy to grow and looks very well with the shorter Juliana hybrids. Its flowers may be rich lilac, pure white, purple or pinkish-mauve so all their colours are harmonious and the contrast in form is pleasing too. There are several other very elegant primulas blooming in winter but these need rather more specialized rock garden conditions.

To keep company with the easier primulas mentioned above, *Hepatica triloba* is one of the daintiest of winter-blooming plants. It is small, not more than six inches high, with white-tipped stamens decorating the round bright lavender-blue flowers. These show their eagerness to open by pushing up just ahead of the leaves in February and March. There is also a charming white-flowered variety.

Equally impatient to bloom is the slightly taller *Pulmonaria angustifolia* 'Munstead Blue', with heads of intense blue flowers something like cowslips appearing before the foliage in February. *P. saccarata*, the Bethlehem sage, follows hard on its heels and is a small rainbow in itself, with harlequin bunches of rose and blue flowers set off by white-spotted green leaves. This plant grows about a foot high.

Symphytum grandiflorum is a low-growing plant which begins to bloom in February. It is used as ground cover but unlike the attractive but pernicious *Petasites fragrans*, it does not usually get out of hand. This small cultivated comfrey grows about nine inches high and its clusters of red-tipped buds open to hanging cream-coloured flowers which show up well above the dark green leaves.

Bergenias, which used to be called megaseas, are also ground-covering plants. They were neglected for a time but are very popular again now for several reasons. Not only are they long-lived, but their tough, cabbagey, evergreen leaves colour richly in winter and look distinguished in flower arrangements. The conspicuous flower heads are beautiful too and these appear from February until April. *B. crassifolia* is a common early-flowering species, with dense rosy-pink blooms. *B. cordifolia purpurea*, with taller and more graceful flower sprays, has purple tints in both flowers and leaves.

Coming now to the round-faced flowers, the first of these to appear is *Adonis amurensis*, whose wide-eyed, yellow blooms have a glistening buttercup sheen and are surrounded by finely cut ferny leaves. There are both single and double varieties of this plant and the double form, a neat dwarf about six inches high, is much more widely stocked by the nurserymen. It flowers in March.

Doronicum, the leopard's-bane, begins to bloom soon after the adonis. *D. cordatum* is another six-inch high beauty, with flowers like yellow marguerites, and *D. austriacum* is a taller plant, reaching eighteen inches, with similar bright and beaming daisies opening from March onwards.

Hacquetia epipactis (*Dondia epipactis*) is an oddity for the rock garden during March, appearing with a green ruff round the fluffy yellow centres of its flowers. The first time I saw this plant I thought birds had pecked off the flowers because they appeared to be lying on the ground, stemless and leafless. But now I know *H. epipactis* must have its little joke and that by the time the foliage has unfolded, its flowers will be riding on top of four-inch stems.

Draba, the whitlow-grass, is a better-known rock plant which blooms in March. *D. aizoides* is a popular species for growing in paving and, with small, clustered flowers held two or three inches above the neat hummocks of foliage, it looks like a bright yellow miniature Thrift.

In late February, and March too, the cushion-forming saxifrages begin to be starred with flowers and they give us a first glimpse of the approaching spring pageant. *Saxifraga apiculata* has small heads of primrose-yellow flowers. It is an easy saxifrage to grow and one of the first to bloom. *S. burseriana* has much larger yellow or white flowers carried singly on bright red stems and it is very showy indeed. *S.* 'Faldonside'

is descended from *S. burseriana* and its creamy-primrose
flowers look particularly lovely above small spiny rosettes of
blue-green foliage. *S.* 'Cranbourne' is another handsome, large
flowered hybrid with silvery-pink flowers and *S. irvingii* is a
lower-growing hybrid with pink flowers above tiny grey

31. *Saxifraga burseriana*

cushions of leaves. *S. oppositifolia* is one of our native plants
which takes to the rock garden and when it is growing well
mats of small bright green leaves will flow round stones,
almost hidden beneath the rosy-purple flowers. There is a
fine garden form of this saxifrage with crimson flowers and
pink or white varieties are on the market too.

BULBS

Bulbous plants contribute some of the showiest flowers to the
winter garden and, planted among deciduous shrubs, they pay
for the shelter they receive with bright splashes of colour.
From January onwards there are many bulbs to choose from
but in the early winter months we are dependent on the crocuses.

Several species of crocus bloom from late autumn until mid-
winter and open wide in every gleam of sunshine. They are all
smaller and more frail-looking than the familiar, spring-
blooming crocuses, but most of them produce a good many
flowers from each corm and some species increase very fast

indeed, advancing across bare ground like little armies of spearmen.

Planted in bold groups these crocuses will extend the coloured carpet already provided by low-growing heaths. *Crocus asturicus purpureus*, blooming in November and December, has deep purple flowers with scarlet stigmas, and *C. longiflorus* is a very sweet-scented lavender-coloured crocus blooming at the same time. *C. laevigatus fontenayi* begins before the end of November. Each corm produces several flowers and they remain in bloom until late January. The flowers are rosy-mauve inside and the backs of their petals are streaked with darker colour. *C. imperati* is another crocus blooming from late November onwards and its parti-coloured flowers are bright violet inside while the outside is quite different, a light buff streaked with black. The contrast between the open flowers and tight buds on a sunny day is both pretty and unexpected.

C. sieberi is a long-lasting crocus which opens its lilac flowers in January and continues for a good many weeks. There is a deeper coloured variety called 'Violet Queen' and the two together make outstanding patches of colour. Smaller and more delicate-looking, the buds of *C. tomasinianus* push up like wax crayons in February and open to fragile starry flowers of pale lavender. This prolific little plant is a tremendous colonizer and is better kept away from less-vigorous crocuses. There are several good purple varieties of *C. tomasinianus*, all of them very charming and free-flowering. *C. chrysanthus* also blooms in February and looks a little more substantial than *C. tomasinianus*. Its many famous varieties cover a wide colour range and give us the first sight of white, yellow, mauve, and violet crocuses all blooming together.

C. 'Yellow Mammoth', the first of the larger crocuses, is not far behind *C. chrysanthus* and in later March all the rest of the garden forms spring up, looking perfect giants now we have become accustomed to the little crocus species blooming so bravely all winter.

The other bulbous plant which blooms in relays from autumn until spring is the hardy cyclamen. *Cyclamen neapolitanum* comes to the end of its flowering period just about the time when autumn changes to winter. A week or two after its last pink shuttlecocks have faded, the pink, white, or deep carmine flowers of *C. orbiculatum* begin to appear and they usually continue until March. The foliage of this charming little cyclamen is neither so plentiful nor so conspicuous as that of *C. neapolitanum* but, like the autumn-blooming plant, it will colonize bare ground under deciduous trees.

Snowdrops are also happy under trees where the shade is not too dense. They make an unforgettable picture above a carpet of fallen leaves, when the white flowers hang above their glaucous green tufts of foliage. *Galanthus nivalis* is the common snowdrop which will grow wild in this way. It blooms from late January until March and fully deserves its title of 'Fair Maid of February'. There are a number of other species available for the garden, most of them less invasive than *G. nivalis*, and there are also a great many varieties. All these snowdrops are attractive, with their different green markings, and some are much larger in all their parts than the four- to six-inch tall common snowdrop, but none is more beautiful. Even the double flowers of *G. n.* 'Flore Plena' seem to me less elegant in their bunchy petticoats than the single flowers of *G. nivalis* itself.

Less well known than the snowdrops, *Leucojum vernum* is the spring snowflake which blooms at the same time. The two plants are rather similar. The flowers of both are white, drooping, green-tipped bells and each plant grows about six inches high but the snowflake has several flowers on each stem.

Eranthis hyemalis, the winter aconite, looks like a buttercup dressed in an Elizabethan ruff. Growing four inches high, it opens its bright yellow flowers very early in the year, but only if the surroundings suit it. In some parts of the country, notably in East Anglia, winter aconites run wild and take to the woods with the snowdrops, while in other districts they have to be coaxed to grow at all. Apart from East Anglia, I remember coming upon a golden colony of them in an East Lothian garden, which is much further north, so perhaps they

32. *Galanthus nivalis*, the snowdrop (left) and *Leucojum vernum*, the spring snowflake

like something in the east coast air. There are several other species of eranthis on the market with rather taller stems and larger flowers.

One of the joys of the early bulb flowers is the diversity of their shapes. Even the ubiquitous daisy-shape can be seen in February and March, when two bright little anemones beam up at us. The four-inch high *Anemone blanda* usually comes first, followed by the slightly taller *A. appenina*. Both have round-faced, bright violet-blue flowers and attractive, deeply-cut foliage which appears just before the flowers and fades away again quite early in the summer. Good white and pink forms of these anemones are also available, along with some washed-out pinks, so they should be seen in bloom before being bought.

The small winter-blooming irises give us still another distinctive flower shape combined with rich colour. They are all stocky little plants when in bloom, with large flowers on strong stalks. The flowers themselves are exceedingly frost resistant and the plants are hardy, but if they are to become established they need a sunny position where the bulbs can ripen properly during the summer. One of the first to bloom, in late January or February, is *Iris histrioides* 'Major'. A magnificent little plant, it has truly heraldic colours. The flowers are bright violet-blue with fuzzy golden tongues on patches of white. *I. danfordiae* follows close behind *I. histrioides* and has rather stumpy, less-graceful flowers redeemed by their glistening lemon-yellow colour. This iris nearly always disappears after flowering for one season, not because the plant has died, but because it breaks up into tiny bulblets after blooming and has to build these up to flowering size before giving another display. How long this takes I cannot say, for all the gardeners I know who like *I. danfordiae* simply treat it as an annual and buy fresh bulbs every year. In February *I. reticulata* opens its slim and elegant flowers. These are a deep velvety purple enlivened with an orange blotch and they smell sweetly of violets. This is a very popular iris and the long string of its named varieties covers many colours from pale blue to rich wine-purple.

The widow-iris, *Hermodactylus tuberosus*, used to be called *Iris tuberosa* and its other common name is snake's-head iris, but under any name it is a beautiful and unusual plant. The flowers are dramatically coloured, pale green and sooty-black. They grow on twelve-inch stems and open in February and March.

33. *Hermodactylus tuberosus* (*Iris tuberosa*), the snake's-head or widow
iris

A plant which has suffered even more changes of name is the
one now called *Ipheion uniflorum* but still to be found in
catalogues under brodiaea, milla, or triteleia. This charming
plant has starry, white or pale-violet flowers, delicately striped

34. *Ipheion uniflorum (Triteleia uniflora)*

with darker colour down the centre of each petal. They grow on four- to six-inch stems among grassy foliage. The main flush of flowers opens in March or April but established clumps produce odd blooms on and off all winter. The flowers are sweet-scented but the cut stems smell strongly of onions and can be rather disconcerting if they are brought indoors to be shown off.

Many of the loveliest and most vivid of all the blue flowers

we can grow are to be found among the dwarf bulbs blooming
in late winter. All five bulbs mentioned below can be closely
planted in large groups to provide sheets, or more modestly,
patches of brilliant colour from February to the end of March.

The dwarf scillas, or squills, come first, pushing through
the ground and beginning to bloom all in one breath, and they
are often in time to keep the snowdrops company. All have
several starry flowers grouped on short stems. *Scilla siberica*
grows about four inches high and is an intense, almost dazzling
blue, with a good cluster of stems from each bulb. *S. s.* 'Spring
Beauty' is a very robust, taller form blooming a little later
than *S. siberica. S. bifolia* is a deeper blue with rather fewer
spikes of flowers. There are exquisite white forms of both these
scillas and less attractive pinks.

Puschkinia scilloides, as its name suggests, is very like the
dwarf scillas. It is a dainty plant but much less strongly
coloured, with very pale mauve flowers striped with darker
mauve in the centre of each petal.

Chionodoxa, the 'glory-of-the-snow', is also very similar to
the scillas. *Chionodoxa sardensis* is the most vivid blue species,
with a tiny white eye. *C. lucillae* is a less striking colour, more
violet-blue, but the flowers each have a large white eye. *C.
gigantea* has the same colouring as *C. lucillae* and grows
twice as high to about ten inches. It has larger and more
numerous flowers on each stem. There are pink chionodoxas
too, but, like the pink squills, they are rather wishy-washy
when compared with the rich blue ones.

Hyacinthus azureus is often to be found in bulb catalogues as
Muscari azureum and the plant is, in all but name, a forget-
me-not blue grape-hyacinth, with tiny bell flowers closely
packed into conical heads. These charming little blooms first
appear in February and continue into March. *H. azureus* is
not only earlier but a good deal cheaper to buy than the light
blue species of muscari, which bloom in April. There is also
a good pure white form of *H. azureus*.

The pinkish-violet flowers of *Tulipa pulchella humilis* make
a pretty foil for any of the small blue flowers we have just
been considering. This tulip is a real dwarf, not more than

four inches high. It blooms in February and needs a sheltered, sunny, well-drained spot if it is to do well. *T. kaufmanniana* is the waterlily tulip, which blooms in March. Its flowers are creamy-white inside and the backs of the petals are boldly coloured with pink and deeper yellow, so this tulip looks striking whether the flowers are open or not. It grows six to eight inches tall and the resemblance to a waterlily comes when the flowers are wide open in the sun. There are a great many beautiful garden forms of this tulip, which all bloom in early spring.

35. *Chionodoxa* and *Anemone blanda*

Narcissus bulbocodium, the hoop-petticoat daffodil, is the bulb to plan for extensive drifts of bright yellow flowers in very early spring, as everyone knows who has seen the Alpine lawn at Wisley in March. There are many varieties of *N. bulbocodium* which have given rise to even more numerous hybrids, but the distinctive feature of all these graceful little daffodils is the flaring, wide-open trumpet.

Those of us who prefer daffodils with more conventional trumpets can grow the deep yellow Tenby daffodil, *Narcissus obvallaris*. This sturdy little plant, not quite a foot tall, colonizes well in grass and blooms very early. It is one of our two native species and the easier to obtain from bulb merchants. The other is *N. pseudonarcissus*, which is even shorter-stemmed and

36. Low-growing winter flowers, *Crocus tomasinianus* and *Hepatica triloba*

is a charming little daffodil, with a bright yellow trumpet and a paler perianth. Among the cyclamineus hybrid daffodils there are some alert-looking ones with pricked-up ears. Two of these attractive plants are 'February Gold' and 'Bartley' (also called 'Peeping Tom' by some) both growing just over a foot tall and blooming in late February or March.

Chapter Seven

Protective Walls, Fences, and Hedges

For the comfort of winter gardeners, protective walls, fences, and hedges are as important as serviceable paths and, when we consider not ourselves but the plants we hope to grow, their shelter becomes of even greater importance. The number of plants able to thrive in a windswept garden is very small indeed but when protection is available our choice of plants becomes much wider, even in the coldest parts of the country.

All three kinds of barrier mentioned here give shelter and all have their place in garden design. When a new garden is being laid out, however, or where the planting area is small, walls and fences have several advantages over hedges.

To begin with, they give immediate protection and privacy, while a successful hedge must be grown from quite small plants and takes several years to reach a useful height. Next, a wall or fence needs much less ground space than a hedge, and it takes no nutriment from the soil, two important points to consider when planning a small garden. A hedge, too, must be trimmed or pruned at intervals but fences and walls need no such attention. Lastly, fences and walls can be used both to support and to protect climbing plants which are on the border-line of hardiness.

A CHOICE OF WALLS AND FENCES

There are a great many ways of building garden walls and fences so the design chosen should be in keeping with the style and size of the garden concerned. Before erecting boundary walls and fences, particularly in urban districts, it is wise to make sure that the local authority will have no objection to the kind of structure proposed. Maximum heights for boundaries are often governed by local bye-laws and there may be other restrictions.

Stone, brick, and concrete walls are usually more expensive than fences but once built they are permanent structures needing no time or money spent on their upkeep. As shelter for the garden and the gardener is the subject of this chapter, low ornamental and retaining walls do not concern us here.

Solid walls five feet or more in height give good protection but they are rather overpowering round a small space. This harsh effect can be softened if plants are trained against the walls at intervals. Unless the walls are unusually ugly ones it is not necessary to hide them completely because bricks and stonework make satisfying contrasts, not only with the shapes of plants but with their colours and textures as well. Horizontal wires strained about a foot apart against a wall make an unobtrusive climbing frame on which plants can easily be trained. The wires themselves should be attached to vine eyes or strong hooks plugged into the masonry.

As an alternative to a plain wall, openwork concrete blocks can be used, either alone or combined with solid blocks, to build screens of a considerable height. These screens look like stone lace and, without appearing in the least forbidding or heavy, give a good deal of shelter by breaking up the force of the wind. There are several openwork blocks on the market, constructed from various compound materials, and they make very elegant screens, which are strong and permanent in spite of their apparent delicacy.

Walls and fences can often be combined to make efficient barriers. Low walls topped with a wooden trellis or an open-sparred fence provide additional shelter at moderate cost and without a shut-in look. Climbing plants can be grown against any of these openwork structures and the tying in of their shoots is an easy matter.

Continuing the same idea, a low close-boarded fence topped with an open trellis is often preferable to a very high solid fence because the latter looks as severe as an unbroken wall without the wall's strength to withstand gale force winds.

37. A variegated climbing plant, *Parthenocissus henryana*

Another type of fence consists of woven panels between solid uprights and this gives good protection while offering less wind resistance than a close-boarded fence, because some air passes through the spaces in the weave. Osier hurdles are a very old and well-tried type of woven fencing material. Many newer types are made from pliable, ribbon-like strips of sawn timber. Both home-making and gardening magazines advertise a wide choice of these and other kinds of fencing panels.

The cheapest fences are naturally the more open ones, but even they give some shelter. Rustic or bark-covered timber makes trellis fences in keeping with a country setting, while palisade fences look attractive in either town or country. Painted white, they help to brighten a shady garden.

Metal, wood, or concrete posts and several strands of wire make a useful open fence for marking boundaries cheaply and unobtrusively while a hedge is growing. Wire netting or chain link fencing can be attached to the straining wires to keep out animals and to lessen the force of the wind. This type of fence can also be used as a support for perennial climbers. The starry-flowered *Clematis montana* or *Vitis coignetiae*, a colourful vine, will speedily turn a wire fence into an ornamental hedge.

Cleft chestnut fencing is sometimes used for marking boundaries but it has little to commend it apart from cheapness. It could not be called either attractive or unobtrusive, nor is it satisfactory as a support for plants.

PLANTING AND AFTER-CARE OF YOUNG HEDGES

Hedges are composed of living plants and, like all plants, these need adequate supplies of air, food, and water at the roots if they are to remain healthy and make good growth. This very obvious fact is all too often overlooked and some gardeners treat hedges like lifeless fences. The preliminary work before planting a hedge is not complicated but there is a little more to it than just stretching a cord across an uncultivated plot to mark a straight line.

People who start hedges off in this way are nearly always disappointed with their progress. What they forget is that hedging plants spend all their lives not only on one spot but in close proximity to their neighbours, so that thorough digging, cleaning and enriching of the ground before planting is even more important for hedges than it is for shrubs which are set out singly. Good soil preparation ensures that plants have a supply of food to draw upon, that they are not forced to compete with perennial weeds for this food and that their roots do not suffer from inadequately drained or too dry a soil.

The site for a hedge should be double dug and enriched with compost and bonemeal. Bulky compost should be buried well down in the second spit so that it will not come in contact with the roots at planting time. Ideally, a strip of ground three to four feet wide, extending on both sides of the planting line, should be cultivated. Although this appears to be a very large area compared with the root spread of the plants when they are set out, its preparation will pay dividends in later years. When a hedge is to be grown against a solid wall or fence the plants should be put in at least eighteen inches away from it to allow them to grow normally and to receive their share of rain.

After planting, a young hedge should be treated in the same way as any other group of new shrubs. In a windswept situation a new hedge can be given the support of a temporary post and wire fence. Only one or at most two wires are necessary but each shrub in the row should be tied to the wire. Evergreens should be sprayed with water at intervals until they have had a chance to take hold and in wintry weather plants which are lifted by frost should be trodden firm again.

Many young hedging plants fail because their roots are allowed to dry out during their first summer after planting and they should be given a thorough soaking with the hose during hot dry spells. Hedges also appreciate a mulch of well-rotted compost spread over the whole rooting area, not only in their first summer but in subsequent years. If the mulch is spread after watering or after heavy rain it will do a lot to conserve moisture in the ground.

A 'formal' hedge is one trimmed with mathematical precision into a dense wall of foliage, an 'informal' hedge allows each shrub in the line to grow more or less naturally and is only lightly pruned to remove worn-out wood or to keep it within bounds. Most small-leaved formal hedges may be trimmed over with shears but to keep large-leaved shrubs neat they are best pruned with secateurs. Large leaves look ugly if they are slashed with shears and they often turn brown.

A well-grown hedge of any kind is dense and twiggy from ground level and bushy young plants are the best for making thick low growth. Leggy specimens may never thicken up into satisfactory shrubs. Many mature hedges need only light trimming but most young hedges should be pruned more severely during their first growing seasons as this builds a good framework of branches and helps to keep them leafy at the base.

THE CHOICE OF HEDGING PLANTS

It is important to choose the right kind of plants for our
hedges because one which really suits its environment can be
a beautiful garden feature as well as a useful shelter or division.
A good choice can also result in a more labour-saving garden.
Where a dwarf hedge is required, plants of normally low
stature are more satisfactory than taller-growing plants,
which need frequent cutting back to keep them at the right
height and which may become bare and woody in consequence.
There are several varieties of lavender, for instance, which
form bushy hedges between one and four feet tall or we might
choose the newer *Berberis thunbergii* 'Erecta' to make a three-
foot hedge with a natural spread of not much more than twelve
inches.

Beech, hornbeam, privet, and yew all accept hard trimming
and can be trained into dense, narrow hedges when necessary.
For a restricted space it is better to choose one of these well-
tried formal hedging plants rather than any of the flowering
and berrying shrubs, which make such lovely hedges when they
can grow freely but which cannot be clipped without the
sacrifice of most of their beauty.

Informal hedges should not be attempted unless the top
growth can be allowed a spread of at least three or four feet.
One of the pleasantest little gardens I have ever visited was
saved by its flowering hedge from being a dull back yard. This
hedge, a tall one of *Cotoneaster lacteus*, bounded three sides of
a gravelled rectangle. On the fourth side, against the house, was
a paved space just wide enough to hold a white painted bench
and two matching plant tubs. The tubs were kept filled with
flowers from spring to autumn, first daffodils and polyanthus,
then petunias, then small chrysanthemums. As the hedge was a
mass of white blossom in early summer and carried its red,
rather rowan-like, berries among the evergreen foliage well
into the winter, this uncluttered little garden looked gay for a
very long season every year. A similar plan could be carried
out to make a secluded corner in part of a larger garden.

Evergreen shrubs naturally remain more dense in winter

than leaf-losing shrubs, but a deciduous hedge which is well trained in its early years grows into a close thicket of stems and gives almost as much protection as the evergreens. It is more important to make a distinction between quick- and slow-growing shrubs and our choice of plants will depend upon the kind of hedge we want. Most quick-growing shrubs make a thin, comparatively short-lived screen. The slower-growing shrubs, on the other hand, tend to be naturally closer in their

38. Four hedging shrubs: holly, yew, beech, and privet

habit of growth and to live longer than their speedier cousins.

I have already pointed out that hedges take up more ground space than walls and fences. Even a narrow foliage hedge whose top growth is restrained by constant clipping has a considerable root spread. Allowance must be made for this, particularly when the hedge stands at the back of a flower border. Where the border is a wide one it is a good idea to set a row of stepping stones between the hedge and the next row of plants to make the hedge accessible for trimming and to prevent too many root systems disputing the same strip of ground.

PROTECTION FOR WINDSWEPT GARDENS

In a windswept position hedges and groups of shrubs are more efficient than high walls as a first line of defence. Solid walls and fences send wind currents up and over them but all the force of the wind comes sweeping down again beyond a comparatively narrow protected strip. Shrubs and trees allow the wind to pass but break up its force.

In the most exposed situations of all an unbroken hedge may be torn down by the wind. More protection can be given by planting a windbreak of tough shrubs in two or more staggered rows, depending upon the amount of ground available. A deep barrier of this kind will filter the wind and take away its cutting edge before it can reach the vulnerable heart of the garden where more tender plants are grown.

A list of plants suitable for all kinds of hedges and windbreaks can be found in Chapter Eight.

Chapter Eight

Plants for Protective Hedges and Windbreaks

This list contains many shrubs and trees which are attractive in winter but others mentioned are summer-flowering beauties and are included for their usefulness in providing shelter. The list also contains a number of shrubs for low hedges. Although not tall enough to shelter people walking about, these low hedges will protect less hardy plants and they can be combined with a taller windbreak on the boundaries of the garden to give more efficient shelter than a single line of defence.

As a general rule the plants for a formal clipped hedge are put in close together, from one to two feet apart. The plants for an informal flowering or fruiting hedge should be spaced at slightly less than their mature width apart to allow the branches to interlace without overcrowding.

Acer campestre (**field maple**). Deciduous. Does well on chalk. A bushy shrub or small tree. The foliage and young growths are pink and maroon in spring, the leaves clear yellow in autumn. It may be grown as a trimmed hedge or as a tall windbreak. Trim in winter. Unpruned trees grow between twenty and thirty feet high.

Acer platanoides (**Norway maple**). Deciduous. Grows in any soil that is not excessively wet. A large, fast-growing tree for screens and windbreaks. It can stand sea winds. Several varieties are available, all with attractively shaped leaves colouring well in spring and again in autumn. 'Crimson King' has deep crimson-purple foliage all summer. Norway maples grow between twenty and thirty-five feet high.

Arundinaria (bamboo). Evergreen. This genus has been much split up, but most nurserymen still list bamboos as *Arundinaria*. They grow best in moist but not stagnant soil. They are hardy but not suitable for very exposed sites. Bamboos make dense clumps of tall jointed canes with slender, fluttering leaves. The plants may live for many years without flowering but after flowering they usually die, leaving gaps, so bamboos are better in groups than as a continuous hedge.

Pseudosasa japonica (*Arundinaria japonica*) is the best-known bamboo in this country and is suitable for most good garden soils. Erect canes arch at the tips. Grows twelve feet high.

Sinarundinaria nitida (*Arundinaria nitida*) is a more graceful plant with arching purple-tinged canes. It is not a rampant grower, reaching ten to twelve feet in height.

Aucuba japonica (Japanese laurel). Evergreen. Thrives in all soils and in sun or shade. Does well in towns and at the seaside. It makes a dense bush with tough, glossy foliage and both green-leaved and variegated varieties are available. Female forms carry large bright red berries. Grows ten feet high but may be kept much lower by pruning in May.

BAMBOO – see Arundinaria.

Berberis (barberry). Many species of Berberis make splendid boundary hedges, as they are hardy, dense and very spiny shrubs. They grow in any soil that is not waterlogged and thrive in sun or shade.

Berberis darwinii. Evergreen. Tiny, holly-like leaves and apricot-orange flowers. A favourite hedge plant, as it stands clipping well and can be kept to one foot in width. Will attain five feet in height in five years. Plant one and a half to two feet apart for a formal hedge.

Berberis gagnepainii. Evergreen. Dense, erect shrub. Has long spines and makes an impenetrable hedge. Pendant yellow flowers and attractive narrow leaves with wavy edges. Grows eight feet high.

Berberis julianiae. Evergreen. Another good screening plant

with dense growth. Scented yellow flowers in early summer.
Grows nine feet high.

Berberis stenophylla. Evergreen. Flourishes even in polluted
atmosphere. Splendid for an informal hedge. Golden flowers on
gracefully arching stems in April and May followed by purple
berries with greyish bloom. Prune after flowering if necessary.
Makes a hedge six feet thick and grows eight feet tall.

Berberis thunbergii. Deciduous. Scented yellow flowers in
early summer, slender bright red berries in autumn. The small
green leaves turn orange and scarlet in autumn, making a
brilliant show. Prune in winter. Grows four to five feet high.

B. t. 'Atropurpurea'. A variety with reddish-purple summer
foliage which also turns to glowing reds in autumn.

B. t. 'Erecta'. A slender upright-growing variety very
suitable for dwarf hedges. It grows one to one and a half
feet thick and two and a half to three feet high. Foliage similar
to the type.

Berberis wilsonae. Deciduous. Small, grey-green leaves turn
bright orange and red in autumn. Clusters of coral-red berries
add to its beauty at this time. Makes a dwarf hedge two feet high.

BLACKTHORN – see *Prunus spinosa*.

BOX – see *Buxus sempervirens*.

BROOM – see Spartium.

Buxus sempervirens (common box). Evergreen. Grows in
sun or shade. A wild plant of chalk hills. The small leathery
foliage is dense and slow-growing. Takes hard clipping well
and is often used for topiary work. Suitable for both low and
high hedges. Unpruned it can make a tree up to thirty feet
high.

Carpinus betulus (hornbeam). Deciduous. Thrives on heavy
clay or chalky soil. A good windbreak for exposed positions.
Hornbeam resembles beech in the shape of its leaves and in its
habit of growth. The foliage is bright green in spring and golden
in autumn. Stands hard clipping well and may be grown as a
narrow formal hedge or as a tall windbreak. Plant one and a

half feet apart for hedges. Trim in winter or late summer.
Unpruned trees grow forty-five feet high and more.

39. *Chaenomeles*, the flowering quince, in fruit and flower

Chaenomeles speciosa (*Cydonia japonica*). Is the flowering
quince. Deciduous. Grows in most garden soils. A spreading
and much-branched shrub with bright green leaves and clusters
of flowers in March and April. The flowers are like apple
blossom and may be white, pink, or red. Golden quinces hang
long on the bushes in autumn and winter. For informal hedges.

Prune if necessary after flowering. Plant three feet apart. Grows six feet high.

***Chamaecyparis lawsoniana* (Lawson cypress).** Evergreen conifer. Grows in most soils and in sun or shade. A quick-growing windbreak for exposed positions. Stands clipping well. This widely planted conifer has fresh green foliage, flattened branches and small cones. It will form a comparatively narrow screen twenty to twenty-five feet high and five to six feet thick. There are many beautiful varieties. *C. l.* 'Allumii' has glaucous blue foliage and grows about a foot a year. 'Fletcheri', a slower-growing plant, also has blue-grey foliage. 'Lanei Aurea' has dense golden foliage. All these varieties can be trimmed.

CHERRY PLUM – see *Prunus cerasifera.*

Choisya ternata. Evergreen. Grows in any soil and in sun or shade. Does well in towns. A bushy shrub with elegantly shaped leaves and clustered heads of sweet-scented white flowers from April to June. For an informal hedge. Straggling shoots can be cut back in July and September. Grows about six feet high and five to six feet wide.

Cotoneaster. A genus of decorative and very hardy shrubs noted for their display of berries in autumn. Will grow in all kinds of soils and in sun or shade. Some species are deciduous and some are evergreen. Those mentioned here are just a few of the large number which make excellent hedges and taller screens.

C. franchetii makes a beautiful hedge. It has greyish evergreen foliage and bright orange-red berries.

C. frigidus is a semi-evergreen forming a large shrub or a small tree up to twenty feet high. Useful as a windbreak.

C. henryanus is an evergreen with dark green foliage and crimson berries. It quickly makes a good screen up to ten feet high.

C. lacteus has leathery green leaves with grey undersides and its small red berries hang for a long time in winter. It is another good evergreen hedging plant.

C. simonsii is a quick-growing semi-evergreen. Leaves and berries both become brilliant scarlet in autumn. A very easy-going plant, it stands clipping well and can be kept as a narrow formal hedge. Prune in winter.

Crataegus monogyna **(hawthorn or quickthorn).** Deciduous. Grows in most soils. A very hardy bush or small tree which stands up well to salt-laden gales at the seaside and to polluted industrial atmosphere. Fairly small tough green foliage, white or pink flowers in May and June, followed by deep red berries. May be grown as a formal hedge as it stands clipping well. Plant one foot apart for a cheap and sturdy boundary hedge to keep out animals. Trim in July, and October. Unpruned trees are among the hardiest of windbreaks.

Cupressocyparis leylandii **(Leyland cypress).** Evergreen conifer. A columnar tree with grey-green foliage, this is the fastest-growing conifer in the British Isles. It does well in almost any soil and tolerates both seaside gales and polluted atmosphere. Suitable for tall but not low hedges because of its exceptionally vigorous growth. The hard cutting back necessary to keep a hedge less than six feet tall make the bushes woody and unattractive. Forms a dense screen up to forty feet high. Plant two feet apart for a hedge, eight feet apart in a staggered row for a tall screen.

Cupressus macrocarpa **(the Monterey cypress).** Evergreen conifer. Stands coastal conditions but young specimens may be damaged in severe winters. Quick-growing, with dense bright green aromatic foliage. It has been much planted as a hedge and windbreak in the past but, because it will stand only light clipping and is rather less hardy, *C. macrocarpa* is being supplanted by the Leyland cypress described above.

DAISY BUSH – see Olearia.

Elaeagnus pungens. Evergreen. Grows in most soils. Stands up to seaside conditions. Both green and gold-variegated varieties can be used for dense bushy hedges and windbreaks. Grows eight to fifteen feet high.

Erica mediterranea. Evergreen. Tolerates lime. A compact shrub with very small, dark-green leaves and rosy-red, honey-scented flowers from March to May. Makes a low, bushy hedge three to four feet high and about two feet wide. *E. m.* 'W. T. Rackliff' is a fine white-flowered variety growing slightly lower.

Erica terminalis (Corsican heath). Evergreen. Tolerates lime. Another good erica for a low hedge. The Corsican heath blooms in late summer. Its rose-pink flowers fade to brown and remain on the plants all winter. Grows three to four feet tall.

Escallonia macrantha. Evergreen. Grows in any reasonably good garden soil and in sun or slight shade. Thrives by the sea. A beautiful free-flowering shrub for informal hedges. It has small glossy deep green leaves and its rosy flowers are produced in summer and autumn. It grows six to eight feet high.

Euonymus japonica. Evergreen. This shrub is not fussy about soil. It thrives on chalk and grows in sun or shade. It can also stand exposure to seaside gales or a polluted industrial atmosphere, and the tough glossy foliage stands clipping well. There are both green and variegated forms of this obliging shrub. It makes a dense formal hedge of any height between three and eight feet or it can be grown unpruned as a windbreak. Plant eighteen inches apart for a hedge.

EVERGREEN OAK – see *Quercus ilex*.

Fagus sylvatica (beech). Deciduous. Beech grows best in light, chalky soils and dislikes heavy damp soil. The leaves are vivid green in spring, russet in autumn. It stands clipping well and may be kept as a slender screen only nine to twelve inches thick. Trim in late July and the dead leaves will be retained all winter. Plant eighteen inches apart. Slow-growing, beech takes six to seven years to form a hedge five feet high. The copper or purple-leaved varieties also make good formal hedges either alone or mixed with green beech.

FIELD MAPLE – see *Acer campestre*.

FIRE THORN – see Pyracantha.

FLOWERING CURRANT – see *Ribes sanguineum*.

Forsythia. Deciduous. Grows in most soils and in sun or slight shade. A very hardy and graceful spring-flowering shrub. The branches are wreathed with yellow bell-shaped blooms in March and April. Best for informal hedges. Stands clipping and becomes dense and twiggy, but when the bushes are kept trimmed most of the flowers are sacrificed. There are several species and varieties to choose from; most grow about eight feet in height and the colour of the flowers ranges from pale greenish-primrose to deep yolk-of-egg yellow.

Fuchsia magellanica **'Riccartonii'.** Deciduous. Prefers a moist but well-drained soil. Does well at the seaside and is a common hedging plant on our south-western coasts. Not suitable for hedging in cold districts as the bushes often die back to ground level in winter. Scarlet and purple flowers hang all along the branches and open continuously from mid-summer to autumn. Makes a bushy, informal hedge six feet high and four to five feet thick.

GORSE – see Ulex.

GUELDER ROSE – see *Viburnum opulus*.

HAWTHORN – see *Crataegus monogyna*.

HEATH – see Erica.

Hebe brachysiphon or *Hebe traversii* **(veronica).** Evergreen. Grows in most soils and in sun or slight shade. One of the most adaptable of hebes, it thrives at the seaside and does well in towns. Small, neat foliage and white, purple-tinged flowers in June and July. Makes a bushy informal hedge about five feet high.

HOLLY – see *Ilex aquifolium*.

HORNBEAM – see *Carpinus betulus*.

Hippophae rhamnoides **(sea-buckthorn).** Deciduous. Grows in almost any soil and can stand very dry conditions. Hardy, resists sea winds. A good shrub for sheltering hedges and windbreaks. Female plants produce large numbers of bright orange berries which persist after the leaves have fallen. May be trimmed in spring to form a hedge six feet high. Groups of unpruned shrubs for windbreaks grow about ten feet high.

Ilex aquifolium (holly). Evergreen. Grows in almost all soils. Stands polluted atmosphere and sea winds. Does well in sun or shade. A compact shrub or small tree with exceedingly tough, glossy, and spiny foliage. The leaves are dark green in the type but there are many handsome variegated hollies. Berries on female plants are usually bright red but may be yellow. Slow-growing, dense and impenetrable, holly is excellent for formal hedges. It has a neat habit of growth and needs only one pruning a year, in August. Takes six or seven years to make a hedge five feet high. Plant two feet apart.

JAPANESE LAUREL – see *Aucuba japonica*.

LAUREL – see *Prunus laurocerasus*.

LAURUSTINUS – see *Viburnum tinus*.

LAVENDER-COTTON – see Santolina.

Lavendula spica (lavender). Evergreen. For light, well-drained soils and a sunny position. Plants must be cut back immediately after flowering or they become straggly. Well trimmed at this time, it makes a low bushy hedge about three feet high. A great favourite but not particularly long-lived.

LAWSON CYPRESS – see *Chamaecyparis lawsoniana*.

LEYLAND CYPRESS – see *Cupressocyparis leylandii*.

Ligustrum (privet). Semi-evergreen. Stands polluted atmosphere and exposed positions. Quick-growing. The small tough leaves may be dark green or variegated. They hang almost all winter except in very severe weather. A cheap hedge, but one that takes a lot of nourishment from the soil and needs frequent trimming to keep tidy. Two species are commonly planted, *L. ovalifolium*, and *L. vulgare*. Both stand any amount of clipping and if well trained when newly planted make dense formal hedges three to six feet high. Plant eighteen inches apart.

Lonicera nitida. Evergreen. Grows in most soils but is not suitable for very cold districts as patches of foliage wither and go brown in severe weather. Very tiny and compact, dark-green foliage. Quick-growing. Makes attractive formal hedges if trimmed four to six times each season. May become floppy, and bare near the ground if not kept trimmed. *L. n. fertilis* is a rather stiffer and more erect-growing plant.

MAPLE – see Acer.

MEXICAN ORANGE-BLOSSOM – see *Choisya ternata.*

MYROBALAN – see *Prunus cerasifera.*

Olearia haastii (daisy-bush). Evergreen. Grows in most soils but prefers light sandy soil. Thrives in sun or light shade and is particularly good at the seaside. Tolerates polluted air. The round bushes have small oval foliage, green above and grey below, and are covered with white sweet-scented daisy-like flowers in July and August. Makes a compact hedge four to five feet high.

Olearia macrodonta 'Major'. Evergreen. Another excellent shrub which blooms rather earlier than *O. haastii*. Stands sea winds and makes a quick-growing sheltering hedge. The toothed foliage is grey-green and holly-like. Grows about six feet high.

Pinus sylvestris (Scots pine). Evergreen conifer. Grows in any well-drained soil and flourishes in the most exposed positions. It is impervious to salt-laden winds but does not grow well in shade. This rugged and hardy tree makes a sturdy first line of defence for gardens in bleak situations. It has tufts of greyish-green, needle-like foliage and deeply fissured red-brown bark. May be grown in groups as a windbreak or as a tall hedge. Plant eighteen inches apart for a hedge and prune in spring.

Pittosporum tenuifolium. Evergreen. Grows in any good garden soil. Does well at the seaside in mild districts. Small waxy-looking bright green leaves on fine black twigs. A very dainty shrub often grown for the cut-flower trade.

Potentilla fruticosa. Deciduous. Thrives in all soils. Does best in full sun but will accept some shade. A hardy shrub making a dense bush of moderate size with rose-like foliage. There are a number of named varieties suitable for low informal hedges up to four feet high. The very attractive single flowers like small dog-roses are usually yellow or white. They are produced over a long period in summer and autumn. Prune in spring if necessary

PRIVET – see Ligustrum.

Prunus cerasifera (**myrobalan** or **cherry-plum** or **green-glow**). Deciduous. Thrives in most soils, in full sun or slight shade. Bright green foliage and small white flowers in early spring. A fast-growing shrub reaching fifteen to twenty feet in height. It is very good for tall screens, but becomes bare near the ground unless cut back after flowering and not allowed to increase in height by more than three feet each year. It may also be kept permanently at about six feet high and makes a dense twiggy hedge. Plant two feet apart for a hedge. *P. c.* 'Atropurpurea' (*P.* 'Pissardii', the purple-leaf plum or purple flash) is a variety with reddish-purple foliage. These two shrubs are often planted together to make a colourful hedge.

Prunus cistena (**crimson dwarf**). Deciduous. Grows best in heavy soils, in full sun or slight shade. Rich red foliage. White flowers in spring followed by black-purple fruits. A very striking shrub for low hedges. Grows five feet high but accepts hard pruning and may be kept much lower. Annual trimming makes it dense and bushy.

Prunus laurocerasus (**common laurel**). Evergreen. Grows in almost all soils, in sun or deep shade, even under trees. A very hardy shrub with tough glossy green foliage. It can be grown unpruned as a tall and bushy windbreak which will reach twenty feet in height or it can be kept trimmed as a hedge. If hard cutting back is necessary it should be done in June. This is a very easy and moderately fast-growing shrub but one that takes a lot of nourishment from the soil.

Prunus spinosa **(blackthorn or sloe)**. Deciduous. Grows in most soils and thrives in exposed positions. Small green leaves follow the clouds of tiny white flowers which appear in March and April. The angular black branches are armed with spines and the blackthorn makes an impenetrable boundary hedge. Plant twelve inches apart. Prune hard back after flowering. *P. s.* 'Rosea' (Sloepink) is a pink-flowered variety with bronze foliage.

Pyracantha (fire-thorn). Evergreen. Grows in any reasonably good garden soil and in sun or shade. A hardy shrub related to the hawthorn, with spiny branches and glossy dark green foliage. Clustered white flowers in May and June are followed by red or yellow berries. *P. coccinea* 'Lalandii' is the vigorous plant with showy orange-red berries often grown as a wall shrub in towns, but it can also be grown as a hedge and stands clipping well. *P. crenulata rogersiana* is a prettier shrub with very small leaves and a compact but graceful habit of growth. The flowers and bright red berries are very freely produced and it is particularly fine as an informal hedge eight to ten feet high. It can also be kept as a much lower formal hedge by trimming in spring and summer.

Quercus ilex **(evergreen or holm-oak)**. Grows in any soil. It stands exposure to sea winds but is not recommended for the coldest parts of the country. A dense deep green tree with variable foliage. Leaves may have plain or toothed edges and are sometimes spined like holly. Stubby little acorns appear in autumn. The evergreen oak grows about thirty-five feet high and may be planted in groups as a windbreak for coastal gardens. It can also be clipped to form a tall screen.

QUICKTHORN – see *Crataegus monogyna*.

Rhododendron ponticum. Evergreen. Needs lime-free soil. Stands polluted atmosphere and some shade. It is often grown on the edge of woodland. A large bush with leathery dark green leaves and trusses of mauve-pink flowers in May and June. Makes an informal hedge ten feet high and about six feet thick. Straggling shoots may be trimmed in winter.

Rhododendron praecox. Semi-evergreen. For lime-free soil. A rather small hybrid rhododendron with many heads of mauve flowers in February and March. Flowers may be damaged by frost in very cold spells but the bushes are unharmed. Makes a low informal hedge not more than four feet high.

Ribes sanguineum (flowering currant). Deciduous. Grows in most soils and in sun or shade. The rosy hanging flowers light up the whole bush in April and are quickly followed by fairly small fresh green foliage. There are several good pink- and red-flowered varieties of this very hardy and easy-going shrub. All make handsome informal hedges six to eight feet high. May be trimmed after flowering and again in late summer if necessary.

Roses. Deciduous. Many roses, both old and new, make beautiful hedges which are dense and twiggy enough to give some shelter. They thrive in any fairly good garden soil and like an open position. From the modern plants, floribunda roses may be chosen to make one of the most reasonably priced flowering hedges it is possible to grow. Most are between three and four feet high but the very popular 'Queen Elizabeth' grows between five and seven feet high and makes a magnificent show of large clear pink flowers all summer.

The older roses offer a wide choice for hedging. *Rosa chinensis* (China rose) begins to bloom in May or June and continues at intervals until late autumn. There are several varieties of this rose with pink, red, or yellow flowers. They make low hedges about three feet high.

Rosa moschata (musk rose) is a continuous-blooming and very fragrant rose. Makes a dense hedge five to six feet high. There are several modern hybrids in a fine colour range and with semi-double flowers.

Rosa rubiginosa (sweet briar) is a native to Britain found mostly on chalk hills. The single pink flowers are scented but the plant gets its common name from the even sweeter fragrance of the foliage, especially after rain. The stems are fiercely spiny and the shrub has been grown as a hedge for centuries.

Rosa rugosa makes a rounded, fairly dense bush with, in addition to the flowers, attractive yellow autumn leaves and large, colourful fruits. Several hybrids with pink, white or red blooms grow into excellent hedges. 'Conrad F. Meyer' is a particularly sturdy plant, which reaches twelve feet eventually. Its height and its impenetrable red spines make it very suitable for boundary hedges. The silvery-pink flowers begin to open in May and continue for many weeks.

Rosa xanthina 'Canarybird' is a graceful, early-blooming rose with small bright green leaves. Scented yellow flowers like dog-roses appear all along the arching stems in May and June. Makes a very ornamental hedge eight feet high.

Rosmarinus officinalis (rosemary). Evergreen. Prefers light soil and needs a sunny position. A fragrant, small-leaved shrub which grows well at the seaside but is not hardy in the coldest parts of the country. It has narrow, grey-green leaves and small blue flowers in late spring and early summer. Rosemary makes a dense bush six or seven feet high and equally wide. It stands trimming and is suitable for both formal and informal hedges. 'Benenden Blue' is a lower-growing variety with bright blue flowers. It makes a hedge three to four feet high.

Santolina chamaecyparissus or S. incana (lavender-cotton). Evergreen. A small shrub which needs well-drained soil and is best in full sun. In a shady position the shining silver foliage becomes dull green. Tight heads of bright yellow flowers appear in July. Trim after flowering. Old wood can be cut back in April to keep the bushes tidy. Makes a low hedge two feet high.

SCOTS PINE – see *Pinus sylvestris*.

SEA BUCKTHORN – see *Hippophae rhamnoides*.

Skimmia japonica. Evergreen. Tolerates lime but is happier without it. Prefers shade and does well in towns. A neat shrub with glossy pointed oval leaves. Small white scented flowers in tight clusters are followed by conspicuous scarlet berries on female plants. Grows slowly to a dense bush five feet high and three to four feet wide.

SLOE PINK – see *Prunus spinosa* 'Rosea'.

Spartium junceum (Spanish broom). Thrives on most soils and does well at the seaside. Needs a sunny or very lightly shaded position. An almost leafless bush whose green, rush-like stems carry richly scented yellow flowers in July and August. It forms a good windbreak for coastal gardens, growing eight feet high.

Tamarix gallica (tamarisk). Deciduous. This shrub is at home on the coast but it will grow inland in most soils. It needs a sunny open position and is impervious to wind. The graceful branches are covered with bright green juniper-like foliage and plumes of small pink flowers in late summer. It makes a quick-growing windbreak ten feet high or it may be cut back in spring to form a lower hedge. *T. tetrandra* is a very similar free-flowering plant but it produces its clouds of pink blossom in May on the previous year's wood so this species must be pruned immediately after flowering.

Taxus baccata (common yew). Evergreen conifer. Grows in any well-drained soil and in sun or partial shade. Hardy but does not thrive in a polluted atmosphere. The short, dark-green, needle-like leaves are set closely all along the twigs and fleshy red berries are carried on female trees. The doyen of shrubs for formal hedges, yew is dense, slow-growing, and very long-lived. It stands clipping well and has been much used for topiary work. Unpruned trees may eventually grow fifty feet high but are usually lower. Hedges and screens may be kept to any desired height by clipping. The foliage of yew is poisonous and this tree should never be grown where cattle or horses can have access to it. Plant two feet apart for hedges.

Thuya plicata (western arbor-vitae). Evergreen conifer. Grows in any well-drained soil and has glossy green foliage similar to that of the Lawson cypress. A quick-growing tree or shrub for hedges and windbreaks. It stands clipping well and can be trained as a hedge or screen ten to fifteen feet high.

Ulex europaeus 'Plenus' (double-flowered gorse). Evergreen. Does best in dry soils and in full sun. A dense bush whose stout stems are closely covered with rigid green spines. The scented golden flowers are most profuse in April and May but appear on and off all the year round. It makes an impenetrable boundary hedge about six feet high and the same width. May be kept tidy by light clipping after the main flush of bloom is over.

VERONICA – see Hebe.

Viburnum opulus (guelder-rose). Deciduous. Grows in any moisture-retaining soil and in sun or light shade. A tall shrub or small tree whose maple-like leaves colour beautifully in autumn. Flat heads of white flowers in June are followed by translucent red berries which persist for a long time. Makes a tall, informal hedge ten feet or more high. Prune after flowering to keep bushy.

Viburnum tinus (laurustinus). Evergreen. Grows in any fairly good garden soil and flourishes in sun or shade. A dense rounded bush with glossy dark green foliage. Flat heads of small pink and white flowers open continuously from October until April and are followed by blue-black berries. A hardy and easy-going shrub for sheltering hedges eight or nine feet high. Prune after flowering if necessary.

YEW – see *Taxus baccata*.

Chapter Nine

Winter Beauty from Plant Groupings

All the suggestions in this chapter will help to make a garden beautiful in winter, but for the happiest results we must decide upon a system of protective hedges or fences before choosing purely decorative plant groupings. These basic features are dealt with in Chapters Seven and Eight.

We gardeners may rather fancy ourselves as theatrical producers when we begin to plan a lovely show which will run for a whole year, but it is as well to remember that with his plants for actors and his garden for a stage the 'producer-gardener' has to solve a number of tricky problems seldom arising in the theatre.

Convenient though it would be, the garden stage does not revolve, so we cannot secretly build up an entirely new setting for Act II while Act I goes on. We cannot even push a few paths and hedges into different positions during an interval, so all the acts of the garden drama must be played against the same backcloth.

Nor is that the main difficulty. Because only annuals and half-hardy plants are removed from the garden when their usefulness is over, a great many members of our cast must be on stage during the entire performance. This limits the number of actors who can be employed and those chosen must either be versatile enough to take part in several scenes or else have the ability to efface themselves while others are in the lime-light. Among the versatile actors we can count many shrubs which are eye-catching while they are in bloom in the early part of the year and again when their fruits and foliage colour in autumn. The most gifted disappearing artists are, of course, the bulbs whose foliage dies away completely when the plants are dormant.

I have made this little excursion across the footlights to emphasize that although our aim here is to construct a beautiful garden in winter it would be very short sighted to do so at the expense of the show during the rest of the year. We must never forget that the plants for each season will only give good results if they are all fitted in without overcrowding.

The next thing to remember when planning to make a garden attractive all the year round is that during the winter we spend quite a lot of time looking out from the shelter of the house, so distant scenes and long vistas should be laid out with this viewpoint in mind. For the same reason a good proportion of the plants which are beautiful in winter should be grouped where we can see them from indoors.

WINDOW BOXES AND PLANTS AT CLOSE QUARTERS

By making use of window boxes we can bring the garden almost into the house and have a good view of the small bulbs and early-flowering rock plants which are best appreciated at close quarters. As a permanent feature and one that will be admired the whole winter through, these miniatures can be interplanted in window boxes with dwarf conifers, winter-blooming heaths, plain-leaved and variegated hebes, dwarf lavender, gold-splashed forms of *Aucuba japonica* and trailing small-leaved ivies. As a more temporary planting the 'winter cherry', *Solanum capsicastrum*, looks very gay and retains its bright orange fruits for several months.

Young specimens of larger-growing evergreen shrubs can also be used in window boxes for a special display and then transferred to permanent positions in the borders, but this is not to be recommended as a regular practice, because evergreens do not relish transplanting.

Another advantage of window boxes, apart from the good view we get of them from indoors, is that by filling them with peaty, lime-free soil we can grow acid-loving plants in districts where the soil of the open garden is unsuitable. I have seen the long window boxes outside banks in the City of London filled to overflowing with acid-loving pernettyas, whose clustered pink, white, and mauve berries blended charmingly with winter-blooming heaths. Such a lavish display could probably be indulged in only by those gardeners who also happen to be City bankers, but the same grouping is effective on a much smaller scale.

40. A small evergreen shrub with white or coloured berries,
Pernettya mucronata

The plants which do well in window boxes are equally suitable for urns and tubs and similar containers. Where these are used to decorate a terrace or paved area close to the house they can often be admired from indoors while at other times tempting us to step outside for a few minutes when we cannot spend long in the garden.

A wooden wheelbarrow is a useful plant holder for a seasonal display of this kind because it is one of the few 'props' in our garden-theatre that we can move around freely and after the plants have finished their show outside the windows they can be wheeled away to an unobtrusive corner. Heavy old wooden barrows can often be bought quite cheaply at country sales now that light metal ones have been so universally adopted. A shabby appearance does not matter so long as the wheel functions and the wood has not rotted.

To adapt the barrow, first bore a few holes in the bottom of the body for drainage, treat the whole inside with a wood preservative that is harmless to plants and paint the outside with hard gloss paint. A black and white finish looks smart, but any bright colour could be chosen to complement the plants we mean to grow.

Raised beds and rockeries flanking a path round the house are other good spots for seeing the smaller winter-flowering plants with a minimum of discomfort during bad weather. Not only are the plants brought up towards eye-level but we can remain dry shod and have some protection from the house while we are looking at them on cold and windy days.

SHUTTING OUT UNWANTED VIEWS

We do not, of course, spend the whole winter examining individual plants at close quarters, so broad views have to be considered, and perhaps altered, when we are trying to find the best way of planning the garden for winter beauty. After the leaves fall in autumn we can see farther and much more clearly both inside the garden and beyond its boundaries. The opening up of the distance may be pleasant in some ways but not in all. For instance, neighbouring buildings which disappear in summer behind deciduous trees often seem uncomfortably close in winter, while inside the garden itself a long view ending in a muddy and almost empty vegetable patch asks to be cut short at a more interesting point. These examples show that two of the tasks facing the winter gardener are the protection of his privacy and the blotting out of eyesores.

Solid partitions are useful for providing shelter but they

cannot be built much more than six feet high and, while hiding unpleasing sights at or near ground level, they do little to give privacy from the windows of neighbouring buildings. Another disadvantage of high garden walls and fences is that unless they are clothed with growing plants we may find the garden resembles a prison yard and we have only exchanged one eyesore for another.

Tall evergreens are often a satisfactory solution but they have to be planted with discretion. A lofty, unbroken screen of evergreens should not be planted along the southern side of a very small garden for during the winter months, when the sun travels in a shallow curve above the horizon, most of the garden will be cut off from its rays. In this position it is better to plant groups of trees and shrubs rather than a continuous belt and to include some deciduous shrubs which will make a twiggy screen without blocking out all the sunshine. It is often possible to make ugly buildings disappear in this way, not by hiding them completely, but by breaking up their outlines with well-placed groups of trees and bushes.

A point to remember in this connexion is that the nearer the screen is to the viewer the more it will hide. One bushy shrub growing a few feet away from a window or a favourite outdoor seat will blot out as much of the distant scene as a whole row of trees placed farther away, say on the garden boundary.

Within the garden, hedges and shrub borders can be planted for their own beauty and also to hide purely utilitarian features like compost heaps, dustbins, fuel stores, and the rather uninviting vegetable patch already mentioned. Evergreen hedges are handsome, making very efficient screens and windbreaks, but they should not be used to the exclusion of all other attractive hedging plants. A garden partitioned with impenetrably leafy hedges is apt to be a gloomy, shut-in place and a mixture of evergreens with deciduous shrubs gives a more airy and varied effect. The bare red or yellow stems of some of the willows and dogwoods will make brightly-coloured thickets which are quite close enough to obscure eyesores without destroying all sense of distance.

MAKING THE MOST OF CONTRASTS

In the last paragraph I mentioned one winter contrast, the use of shrubs with leafless stems as foils for evergreens. This is a garden adaptation of the unplanned but lovely contrast often seen in winter woods when a holly tree or an ivy-covered trunk takes on an importance unknown in summer and stands out, dark, solid, and gleaming, against the misty grey-browns of leafless twigs. The same woodland setting, too, makes withered beech leaves seem bright as flames among the quieter colours.

We can see another object lesson in the open countryside where fields of grass, bleached stubble, and bare earth join together in a broad patchwork with every colour gaining something from its neighbours. The actual contrast between some of the colours may not be very strong, but it appears so because the scale is large and because each piece of the patchwork has a simple well-defined shape.

This teaches us how to strengthen gentle colours in the winter garden by using bold groups and it also illustrates the restful effect of large, simple shapes. These are just some of the contrasts of colour and shape that can be employed to make separate features of the garden balance and enhance one another.

A lawn stretching away from the house is a very common garden feature and one which makes a pleasant outlook at all seasons, especially when it is bounded by mixed borders of trees, shrubs, and other plants. This scene owes its immediate appeal to the contrast between smooth unbroken turf and the jumble of shapes surrounding it. Contrasts within the borders next play their parts in making the view either more or less satisfying. In summer large bright masses of flowers can easily be arranged to catch the eye, in winter we have to rely more on contrasts of light against dark and dark against light to show finely etched shapes and weaker colours to advantage. The pale and delicate-looking flower sprays of *Viburnum fragrans* or of the autumn cherry, for instance, can be lost against a confused or light-coloured background, but planted in front of a solid dark green conifer the flowers shine out like stars.

The more dominating black and white trunks of silver birches will show up against either dark or strongly coloured backgrounds but for the very best effect their hair-thin, catkin-laden twigs have to be seen against the sky. By planting the trees in front of lower-growing shrubs, a garden wall, or a squat building, we are giving them the kind of background that lets us enjoy all the variations of their magpie colouring.

Two other well-known catkin-bearing trees which look pretty against a pale background are the common hazel, with its tassels of greeny-brown catkins hanging all winter and ripening to yellow very early in the year, and the common alder, with old cones and new catkins carried at the same time on its leafless branches. The alder grows almost as tall as the silver birch but the hazel seldom reaches twelve feet and grows generally as a bushy shrub rather than as a standard tree.

There are very decorative garden varieties of both these trees, notably *Alnus glutinosa* 'Imperialis', an alder with finely-cut leaves, and the corkscrew hazel, *Corylus avellana* 'Contorta'. This has astonishingly twisted branches, as its name indicates. The plant gained an Award of Merit many years ago and is certainly very distinctive in winter, but some people consider it grotesque. 'Like something out of a nightmare', and 'Unhealthy looking!' are two remarks I have overheard when the plant has been exhibited at the Royal Horticultural Society's shows.

Many other deciduous trees have a lacy winter beauty surpassed only by the full glory of their spring or autumn foliage. Although too large a tree for most gardens, the London plane deserves a special mention here for the charm it adds to town streets and squares, not only in summer but also all through the winter, when the flaked trunks and branches are canopied with leafless twigs and airily swinging fruit bobbles.

An unsurpassed group of these trees grows, suitably enough, in Lowndes Square, just south of Hyde Park in London. Anyone interested in tree shapes should go there on a bright winter's day to see the pattern these planes make against a background of tall and massive buildings.

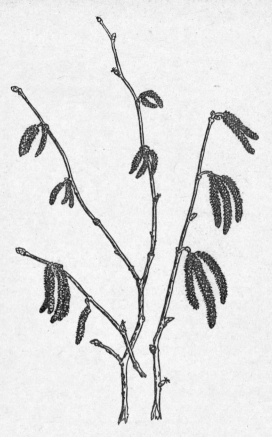

41. A deciduous catkin-bearing hazel, *Corylus avellana*

In addition to such lovely filigree effects, the general outlines of both evergreen and deciduous trees are conspicuous in winter and can be most useful for building up garden pictures. Columnar or spire-like shapes are particularly striking and when they rise from several rounded ones a pleasing contrast results, no matter what individual plants compose the group.

The pattern can be repeated at different levels, beginning with miniature conifers among hummocky and prostrate rock plants and climbing step by step to noble trees that soar thirty or forty feet above thickets of bushy shrubs. *Juniperus communis* 'Compressa' is probably the most popular little upright conifer for adding dignity to the rock garden. It makes a slender, bluish-green cone never more than three feet tall when fully mature. At the other end of the scale the incense-cedar, *Libocedrus decurrens*, can be used with dramatic effect, but is takes a garden of really generous proportions to set off the towering columns of these seventy-foot trees. For less spacious gardens there is a wide choice of medium-sized conifers and a selection of these and of other erect-growing trees will be found in Chapter Five.

PART TWO – CENTRES OF INTEREST

The use of contrasting shapes and colours among the plants chosen is a big help towards banishing dullness from our gardens in winter, but still more can be done by introducing a centre of interest or, in other words, something which stands out from the background and catches the eye. This centre of interest may consist of plants alone or it may include a structural feature such as a pool, a garden shelter or any of the ornaments suggested in Chapter Ten.

Earlier I have stressed that, if a garden is to be colourful all the year round, room must be found for a mixture of plants to follow one another in beauty as the months go by. This does not, however, rule out the grouping together of plants which make a show at roughly the same time. Provided they do not take up too large a share of the garden's total area, a few beds and borders can be given over entirely to plants of one season and this arrangement will help to avoid the thin, spotty effect that can occur if plants are spaced out in a spring-summer-autumn-winter rotation over the whole garden. For full enjoyment the place chosen for a congregation of winter plants should be visible from the windows of the house.

COLOUR AS A CENTRE OF INTEREST

Bold colours are much less common in winter than in summer, but close grouping helps to intensify those available. Yellow is the easiest bright colour to find in any quantity and a concentration of plants with yellow foliage, fruits or flowers makes a cheerful and eye-catching picture against almost any background. As a simple beginning for the group the golden privet should not be despised. It is an easy shrub which is very nearly evergreen and it often carries sprays of pure yellow leaves as well as variegated green and yellow ones.

Elaeagnus pungens 'Aurea Variegata' is probably the gayest of all variegated evergreens. Its very glossy leaves are splashed with daffodil-yellow, it forms a dense bush and, like the privet, is not fussy about soil and will grow in sun or shade. A variegated holly is another possibility and *Ilex aquifolium* 'Golden Queen' is a handsome variety with yellow margined leaves. Despite its name this is a male form and for yellow berries the female *I. a.* 'Bacciflava' can be planted with it.

One or more specimens of a golden-foliaged conifer such as *Chamaecyparis lawsoniana* 'Lutea' could also be included to provide a different shape and texture, while behind any of these the yellow-berried *Pyracantha rogersiana* 'Flava' would make a splendid wall plant. The chaenomeles, or flowering quinces, are other good wall plants carrying their golden, apple-like fruits for a long time.

Dwarf yellow-berried shrubs are almost impossible to find but there are any number of trees and tall bushes which produce bright yellow berries and other fruits. In a large garden room might be made to include the evergreen *Cotoneaster rothschildianus* in the yellow group. This handsome shrub forms a spreading bush ten feet high and almost as much across. Another large bush or an upright-growing tree is the crab-apple, *Malus* 'Golden Hornet'. Both these plants have the advantage of carrying their heavy crops of yellow fruit well into the winter.

The choice of yellow winter flowers is quite wide but, with only the old favourites Chinese witch-hazel, winter jasmine,

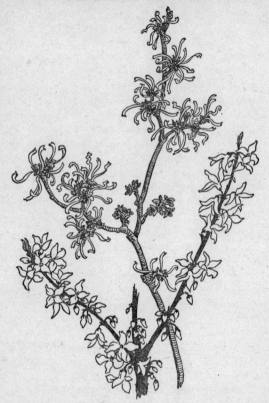

42. **T**wo yellow-flowered shrubs for succession, *Hamamelis mollis*
(in the centre) and *Forsythia intermedia*

and forsythia to supply a succession of starry blooms the
yellow corner would give us a continuous private store of
winter sunshine from October to the end of March. Nearer
ground level the general brightness could be intensified with
plantings of winter aconites, early and late yellow crocuses,
daffodils, and the aptly named pansy, 'Winter Sun'.

A touch of scarlet added to a yellow corner lights it up even
more and to provide this gay contrast a bush of *Cotoneaster*

conspicuus decorus is a good choice. This plant carries an immense crop of bright red berries along its shoots and, as the birds seldom touch them, the berries are a brilliant sight for months.

Another satisfying but quite different winter colour grouping can be achieved by mixing silver-leaved evergreens such as senecios and santolinas with plants bearing white, pink, and purple fruits or flowers. To be entirely successful, the sunniest and best-drained spot must be chosen for this group, because the evergreens will turn from silver to an uninteresting greyish-green in a shaded or damp position.

An island bed in an open stretch of lawn can be a very attractive centre of interest when it is filled with plants in this colour range. As a starting point the snowberry, *Symphoricarpos albus laevigatus*, and *Callicarpa giraldiana* contribute long-lasting white and violet berries respectively, while, in addition, the callicarpa leaves take on pinkish-mauve tints before they fall. The silver-leaved evergreens can be planted round these two shrubs and they will associate well with the various species of ericas, which produce drifts of mauve-pink and white flowers during the winter.

Next, some of the hellebores deserve a place near the front of the bed where their lovely white or plum-purple flowers can be fully appreciated. For a fairly tall flowering shrub to give lightness to the group, either *Viburnum bodnantense* 'Dawn' or the older *V. fragrans* could be included. The first produces a great many rose-pink flower clusters on its bare twigs, the second has pink-tinted buds opening to white and both plants remain in bloom for many weeks during the winter, from well before Christmas until March in some seasons.

Daphne mezereum is another lovely flowering shrub within our colour range. It begins to open its tightly packed reddish-purple flowers in February, just as the snowdrops appear, and at the same time the early *Crocus tomasinianus* can be relied upon to carpet any remaining spaces with fragile lavender or purple blooms.

SPECIMEN TREES

As an alternative to this kind of mixed planting, an isolated ornamental tree can be a pleasing centre of interest, if it is well chosen and well placed. The size and general proportions of the tree at maturity are very important because these must be in keeping with the surroundings. Too small a tree will merely look insignificant, but one which grows too large may swamp a small garden, cause damage to drains and foundations, or cut off light from windows.

Although size is an important consideration it is not, of course, the only one when a tree is chosen for a conspicuous position. It must have some claim to beauty all the year round and weeping trees are popular for this reason. Any distinctively shaped tree can be equally successful, however, provided it fits in well with the character of the garden. A tree which has only a brief period of glory in the spring and then looks drab or untidy for the rest of the year is not the best one to select for this star spot. A much better choice is a tree with several seasons of beauty, for instance, one that blooms in spring and later gives an attractive show of fruit or coloured foliage.

The willow-leaved pear, *Pyrus salicifolia* 'Pendula', is eligible on almost all counts as a centre of interest. Its weeping branches are covered with creamy blossoms in spring, the silvery-green foliage is pretty and the tree produces a great many small yellow fruits. The snowy-mespilus, *Amelanchier canadensis*, is another striking tree both in spring, when clouds of pure white flowers give it its common name, and again in autumn when the leaves colour and the whole tree flames orange and scarlet. Still another white-flowered tree with a second season of interest in autumn is the crab-apple, *Malus* 'Red Sentinel', which has a brilliant display of luminous, red fruit weighing down the branches and lasting almost all winter.

But these are only three examples from a very long list of lovely trees. So many are eye-catching in one way or another that every gardener should be able to find a suitable tree for his particular purpose. For a position on a lawn, however, I should not choose the holly, in spite of its undoubted winter beauty. Its prickly leaves take a very long time to decay and their spiky, dried-up remains can make the grass uncomfortable for lazing or for children playing.

It is not, of course, essential to possess a lawn before we can

43. A winter-blooming plant, *Eranthis hyemalis*, the winter aconite

plant specimen trees. They can be just as happily placed in paved areas and among low-growing plants in a border or on a rockery as they are in grass. What is important is to consider their exact positions carefully in relation to their setting. The precise centre of any kind of clearing is seldom the best spot for a specimen tree. Our eyes will be better pleased if the tree is stationed nearer to one side of the clearing than to the other and also towards one end.

To make an ornamental tree still more of a focal point in winter a succession of bulbs, corms, and tubers can be planted close to it, either just beyond the spread of the branches or, where these are sufficiently high and open, in a bed around the trunk. Several species of autumn crocus and colchicums can be chosen to begin the show with their lilac, purple, or white flowers and the deep rose, hardy cyclamen, *Cyclamen neapolitanum*, will keep them company. Soon after Christmas the winter aconites lead a regular procession of miniature flowers and by the beginning of March the first small daffodils are usually in bloom. We can also buy treated bulbs of some larger and normally later daffodils which will bloom early in February, but if a show of colour is important at this particular time each year it must be remembered that the forcing treatment affects the bulbs' flowering time only in their first season after planting.

GROUPS OF LOW-GROWING PLANTS

Sometimes neither specimen trees nor tall shrubs are wanted but it is still felt that the garden needs a plant group as a centre of interest during the winter. For an open position massed beds of winter-blooming heaths might be chosen, as they can provide a fine expanse of rich colour during the dark months. Although some species will not tolerate a limy soil, others are less fussy and, with the help of top dressings of peat, do well anywhere except below overhanging trees, where they dislike the drips.

On the edge of trees a border filled with bulbs and low-growing evergreens is a pleasing feature and a more interesting one than a bed containing bulbs alone because this can remain a dreary expanse of muddy earth for rather a long time while we wait for the flowers to appear.

The plain green and the yellow-variegated forms of the lesser periwinkle, *Vinca minor*, are attractive ground covers, so is the trailing *Euonymus fortunei* (*radicans*) with purplish or silver-variegated leaves. Both these plants grow little more than a foot tall and another of similar height is *Sarcococca humilis*, a rather stiffer little evergreen with the added attraction of intensely sweet-smelling flowers in February. Most winter-blooming bulbs sensibly grow only a few inches high but if space is left between the evergreens for the bulbs to be planted in bold groups the all-over effect is very colourful and pretty.

If a complete evergreen ground-cover is preferred, prostrate ivies can be planted between the other shrubs and the bulbs allowed to grow through them. There are several very decorative forms of the common ivy, *Hedera helix*, which are suitable. These include 'Buttercup', with small golden-yellow leaves, and 'Jubilee', which also has small leaves and is variegated with green and silver.

SCENTED PLANTS FOR THE WINTER GARDEN

This section would be incomplete without some mention of an invisible beauty of the winter garden – the beauty of sweet scents. A surprisingly large number of winter-blooming plants are perfumed and no one seems quite certain why, because in this country there are very few insects about in winter to be attracted to the flowers. I suppose it must mean that the plants originally came from countries where insects *are* active during the flowering season or that the winter-blooming plants we know are hybrids which have inherited perfume from summer-blooming parents.

Some of the scented flowers are small and not very showy. *Osmanthus ilicifolius*, for instance, has rather privet-like blooms tucked in among its leaves while the sarcococca, mentioned earlier, has inconspicuous little white bells hanging close to the stems. Other shrubs, however, would still be grown for their lovely flowers if these had no scent at all. The Chinese witch-hazels, *Viburnum fragrans* and its hybrids, and *Mahonia japonica* all have brightly coloured, exquisitely shaped blooms and many more sweet-scented winter flowers are just as decorative. My own favourites are first the winter-sweet, *Chimonanthus praecox*, with a scent like narcissus, second

Mahonia japonica, smelling of lily-of-the-valley, and a very close third, *Daphne odora*, whose sweet perfume has a tang of lemon about it. The scent of the daphne remains strong and true for more than a week when branches are cut and brought indoors.

Although the scents of some winter flowers are powerful we have to bend close to others to appreciate them, so it is only sensible to station the plants where they are sure to be noticed.

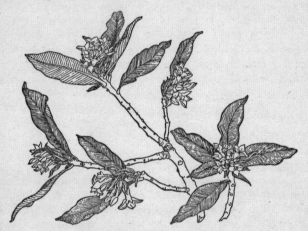

44. A fragrant evergreen shrub, *Daphne odora*

Good positions for scented flowers are near often-used doors, including not only house doors but also the doors of outbuildings such as the garage and fuel store. It is not such a sound idea to put them at a distance from paths or in any part of the garden where it is impractical to walk after rain, for then the flowers may come and go without anyone savouring their sweetness. Perhaps the best position of all for one of these plants is beside a sheltered seat where we can take our ease and add the enjoyment of the flowers' fragrance to the pleasure of winter sunshine.

Chapter Ten

Winter Beauty from Ornamental Structures and Layout

As I said at the beginning of Chapter One, shape is more important than colour in the winter garden. Most plant groupings provide a variety of softly rounded forms and when plants are combined with structural features these can add the stronger, more severe shapes necessary to give the whole layout of the garden a sharper definition.

ACCENT ON LEVELS

We can begin by drawing attention to the contours of the ground itself. Different levels make a garden more interesting and for a pleasantly varied effect it is not always necessary to embark upon large-scale earth-moving operations. Quite often a slight natural slope can be accentuated by marking it with a shallow step, or with a low retaining wall only a few inches high. There is always a certain amount of work in making these structures, of course, but, when they are completed and we see how they emphasize a difference in level which before was scarcely noticeable, our efforts are well repaid. Retaining walls and steps with their definite clean-cut lines always add character to the garden.

Even when we are faced with an utterly flat plot or a paved yard another level can be introduced by building a raised bed inside low walls. Raised beds on a soil base present no problems except that they dry out more quickly than the rest of the garden. Even deep-rooted trees can be grown in them. When beds are built over an impervious surface such as concrete, on the other hand, very deep-rooted plants cannot be grown and care must be taken to prevent the soil becoming stagnant through bad drainage. To avoid this a few small spaces, called 'weep holes', should be left in the lowest course of the retaining walls and the soil in the beds should be placed on top of a drainage layer of gravel or broken brick deep enough to cover the weep holes.

With the exception of openwork screening blocks, all the materials suitable for boundary walls can be used for steps and low walls within the garden. The happiest effect is usually achieved when the material chosen matches the walls of the house itself, the repetition linking house and garden together.

A SPACIOUS LOOK FOR SMALL GARDENS

As time passes and their knowledge of plants increases, most keen gardeners wish for a larger garden than the one at their disposal. Happily, or unhappily, it is seldom possible to move house every few years just to keep pace with our horticultural ideas and if we are to enjoy the gardens we do possess it is best to curb a natural impulse to cram everything in. Although we cannot alter the total area of a garden, both the grouping of plants and the placing of various structural features can change its apparent size and shape. The nicest gardens are arranged to look spacious no matter what their actual size may be. By planning carefully and using a little sleight of hand we can even make our gardens appear larger than they really are.

By far the best way to make a garden look spacious is to keep the layout simple. A quite tiny garden can be successfully planned round one ornamental structure but if statues and bits of masonry greet us on all sides they will only make the garden appear smaller than ever and give it an unfortunate resemblance to a builder's yard. Scaled-down imitations of famous gardens usually fall into this category, because grand designs depending on sheer size and the sweep of land and sky cannot be compressed. Painstaking work will produce a kind of Beaconscot effect certainly, but the average garden is diminished to vanishing point in the attempt.

Simplicity does not, however, mean sameness. Because all the gardens in a street are identical in size and shape is no reason for laying them all out to an identical plan. But every plan chosen should be suitable not only for a plot of that particular size but also for a plot which is one of a row. Each garden is the setting for one house in the street but the whole neighbourhood is the background for the gardens and cannot be completely ignored. This is why the layout we admire round an isolated country cottage may not please us when it is sandwiched between fences and overlooked by other buildings.

Any garden with only a few simply shaped paths and borders appears more spacious than one laid out in a mosaic of small beds and short paths. In the same way, an unbroken stretch of grass always looks larger than a similar area of grass divided by a path. It is not always possible to do without a path but sometimes one can be designed to skirt the grass. Alternatively, stepping stones sunk level with the turf can be substituted for a continuous path across it. Stepping stones are just as effective for taking us dry shod from one spot to another and yet they do not seem to make the lawn shrink, or to separate it into two parts.

Very small lawns are not a success unless they can be kept almost untrodden. Grass quickly wears out if it is constantly used and the bare tracks and bald patches which appear do nothing either to beautify the garden or to make it look spacious. A paved area is more practical and better looking than a shabby lawn where one small piece of ground has to be walked over continually, used as a sitting out place, and perhaps as a children's play area as well.

All straight or gently curved lines going from end to end of a garden make it look longer. When two parallel lines run the length of a narrow plot which is normally viewed from one end we can even make use of mock perspective and, by placing the lines a little closer together as they go away from us, cheat our eyes into believing the plot is longer than it is. Two rows of regularly spaced shrubs can give this optical illusion, so can the sides of a path or a formal pool. Alternatively we might use a pergola, twin hedges, or the edges of a long flower bed.

I have also heard it suggested that a dwarf form of some well-known conifer could be planted at the end of a narrowing vista or that a wall of very small bricks could be built there to emphasize the feeling of distance but I have not seen either of these ideas carried out. I think myself that this is attempting to carry the deception rather far and that the scene would only be convincing if no other plant or structural feature were visible in the distance to give the game away.

Oddly enough, another method of making a garden seem larger is by hiding a bit of it from sight. This can be done first of all by marking the garden boundaries unobtrusively and, by allowing the eye to travel on unchecked, incorporating into our own garden a view of our neighbours' trees or a stretch of open countryside. Even when the boundary exists as a solid fence or wall it can be obscured with a shrub border of varying depth which conceals the exact position of the dividing line and acts as a frame for the more distant landscape. During the winter a view like this is doubly appreciated if it can be seen from inside the house and this should be kept in mind when we are deciding where to place the tallest trees or shrubs and so are shaping the frame for our picture.

When the surrounding neighbourhood does not lend itself to this innocent form of brigandage we can employ a deceptive layout inside the garden instead. This consists of siting a high fence, hedge, or group of shrubs a short distance from the farthest boundary of our own ground. The barricade should cross the garden almost from side to side but still leave room for a path to be seen passing it and disappearing beyond. As most of us possess romantic imaginations, masking the garden's exact dimensions in this way gives an impression of size and of beauties still to be revealed, although in a really small plot the mysterious path might lead only to a parking place for the wheelbarrow or to the compost heap.

SUNTRAP SEATS

In a somewhat larger garden the path we have just been considering could live up to its promise and lead to a sheltered corner where a comfortable seat would make this a popular place on sunny days all the year round. For an ideal sitting-out spot in winter the seat should stand on paving or on a well-drained path among a collection of winter-blooming plants, while the whole corner should be sheltered by high walls on the north and east sides but be open to the south and west. With this layout the coldest winds are kept at bay and frosted plants are protected from the damaging early morning sun, but later in the day, when rising temperatures have melted the frost, both plants and people can enjoy sunshine and reflected warmth from the sheltering walls.

Of course, not every garden can provide such a perfect spot as this for sitting out of doors in winter, but we can often find a sunny corner and improve upon it with temporary screening. A south-facing angle where two fences or hedges come together is usually quite sheltered and, if the hedges are not dense enough to keep off the wind, osier hurdles behind the seat will reinforce them. When no corner is available a seat can be backed up against a wall or a hedge and enclosed at the sides with similar hurdles, or, better still, with corrugated PVC sheeting which, being translucent, keeps out draughts without cutting off the light. Cold and dampness underfoot are just as unpleasant as draughts, so all seats intended for use in winter should stand on a hard surface rather than on grass.

COVERED SHELTERS FOR THE WINTER GARDEN

When the weather is too cold or wet for us to sit in the open it is pleasant to have a seat under cover from which we can look out at the garden. Maximum comfort and protection is given by a glazed porch or house extension which we can reach without going outside at all and which can easily be fitted with some form of heating. Although not exactly greenhouses, these can be used to some extent for the same purpose. A great many house plants do well in them, revelling in the good light, so with a glazed annex we can not only enjoy the view but do a little indoor gardening as well.

A number of firms selling greenhouses and garages also sell

house extensions. They are made in many sizes, all have the largest possible amount of window space and some have transparent roofs. In recent years they have become very popular as a comparatively cheap way of adding another room to the house. Some have to be erected by a professional builder, but others are supplied in sections ready for assembly by the home handyman.

At the Chelsea Flower Show in 1965 one impeccably laid-out garden was designed round a classical rotunda reminiscent of the Temple of Aeolus at Kew. Very beautiful it looked but unmistakably in the grand manner, and of the thousands who stopped to admire I do not think many owners of small gardens went home determined on a do-it-yourself temple. For most of us the ornamental garden can seldom be completely divorced from such mundane features as the clothes line or the vegetable patch. Dustbin, fuel store, garage, and toolshed are often in evidence too, so a homely kind of shelter fits in best.

But if the garden is not particularly formal the shelter need not be conventional either. Quite often in seaside gardens an old rowing boat is sawn in halves and upended to act as a windbreak behind a seat. I have also seen a large-windowed chick-rearing house turned into a very cosy winter sitting-out place with yellow jasmine flowers and red pyracantha berries looking in at the door and, inside, all the comforts of cushioned chairs, a folding table and a paraffin stove.

The most unusual shelter I have ever known, however, was a very small and old single-decker tram. This stood in a half-wild cliff-top garden and was one of my favourite childhood haunts. To adult eyes the little tram probably looked quite incongruous, perching there among the dog-roses, but at least it was not too grand for its setting and what a perfect shelter it made in bad weather. There were two long seats, splendid views, and thick glass windows all round to keep out the wind and rain but to let in plenty of light.

The chief differences between a summer-house and a winter shelter are pinpointed by the choice of both the chick-rearing house and the tram car for use in winter. In summer we want

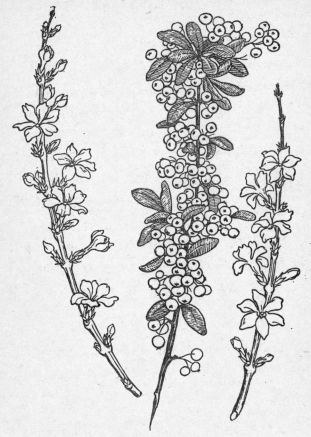

45. Colour in mid-winter: yellow jasmine flowers and (in centre) red pyracantha berries

an open-sided building that screens us from the sun while allowing a free passage of air, but in winter we want to feel the warmth of the sun and yet be protected from wind and cold. An existing summer-house can often be made more comfortable for winter use by tacking clear polythene sheeting over

46. An evergreen with flowers and fruits in autumn, *Arutbus unedo*,
the strawberry tree

open sides or window frames, taking care, of course, not to
make the place completely airtight.

When a new shelter is being erected with the winter garden
in mind, rigid corrugated PVC sheets will make a watertight
roof that lets in sunshine and light. To cut out glare in summer
the roof can either be fitted with blinds or annual climbers
can be trained over the outside. Removable window frames
also help to make a shelter adaptable for all seasons and, if

these are fitted with polythene rather than with glass, they are light to handle and less worrying to store.

GARDEN ORNAMENTS

Apart from its utility, a well-placed garden shelter provides a bold point of interest which combines with plant groupings to make a complete and attractive picture. A variety of garden ornaments can be used in a similar way. To give one example, a statue or a plant container at the end of a long path will please the eye by acting as a punctuation mark, or as a reason for the path ending exactly where it does. Stone, lead, or terra-cotta ornaments all contrast well with plants. Not only are they as pleasant against a background of evergreens and berries in winter as they are among the roses and lilies of summer, but they can take the place of a gay mass of flowers and become the focal points round which the winter display is planned.

Lightweight fibre-glass replicas of antique leaden ornaments can be bought. They are beautiful and weather-resistant productions and much more easily moved around than the originals, but they are not cheap. The many plastic ornaments on sale are much less expensive and, although many are crude, some of the newest are very much better in design, colour, and finish.

For lawns and paved areas, either a sundial or a bird-table makes a particularly suitable ornament because these both need an open position if they are to function satisfactorily. In the shade a sundial cannot show the time, while a bird-table is a safe feeding place only if it is some yards from bushes or any other cover that would allow the birds' enemies to approach unseen.

A regularly supplied bird-table is an engrossing source of interest in winter, for people as well as for birds. 'Regularly' is the important word in the last sentence, so the feeding place should be easy for us to reach in all weathers. This makes a paved area ideal but when a position in the middle of the lawn is chosen a row of stepping stones leading to the table is not only decorative but useful. If we are to enjoy the entertainment fully the bird-table should be visible from the house or from a winter shelter.

Perhaps it is only fair for me to mention here that, since making a birds' feeding place about ten yards from my kitchen window, I have found that all work in the kitchen takes three times as long to do, but that I can now prepare vegetables, make pastry, iron clothes, and wash up almost entirely by touch.

Artificial well-heads are sometimes built over imaginary wells and they can look quite pretty, although rather contrived. Genuine well-heads and pumps, on the other hand, are utterly satisfying as garden ornaments even when the wells they serve are disused. This is probably because in most instances they are very old and, the gardens having grown up around them, they look completely at home in the positions they occupy.

Chapter Eleven

Soil Preparation

All the plants which look decorative in winter are perennials, that is, they should live for years, and once in the garden most of them spend their lives in the same spot, so time taken up with thorough soil preparation is never time wasted. Good drainage is particularly important to plants which are active during the winter, both those grown for their evergreen foliage and those producing winter flowers. Many plants in both these categories can weather severe frosts provided their roots are in dry, porous soil, but if the roots are waterlogged they have a much poorer chance of survival.

The plants are most susceptible to damage during their first winter in a new situation so at this time in their lives a well-drained site is much more valuable than a well-manured one. Good soil preparation and careful planting ensure that new specimens begin to grow as soon as air and ground conditions become suitable and this helps plants to establish themselves in the shortest possible time.

KINDS OF SOIL

There are five main types of garden soil. Some pose more problems for the gardener than others, but they can all be improved with cultivation.

Sandy soils are called 'light', 'warm', or 'hungry' soils. Water drains away quickly from sandy soils and their other good points are speedy warming up in spring and the ease with which they can be dug at all times of year. Their bad points are that they retain insufficient moisture in dry seasons and also that plant foods are quickly washed down beyond the reach of

feeding roots. To improve sandy soils and make them more
retentive well-rotted animal manures, compost, hop manure,
granulated peat, or leaf mould should be dug in.

Clay soils are the exact opposite of sandy soils and are called
'heavy' or 'cold' soils. They are very close-textured and retentive, so they easily become waterlogged and difficult to dig.
Clay soils are rich in plant food but, because of their wetness
and coldness over a long season, they are inhospitable to
plants. Breaking up the subsoil and at the same time digging
in coarse sand or fine gravel will help the drainage of clay
soils and any of the substances mentioned above for improving
the texture of sandy soil will do the same for clay.

Soils containing chalk or other forms of lime are known as
'alkaline'. They are hostile to certain groups of plants, notably
rhododendrons, pieris, pernettya and most heathers. Chalk
soils may be very shallow, so plants in a poor, chalky soil
suffer from dryness at the roots and lack of nutriment along
with excessive alkalinity. Granulated peat tops the list of
useful additions to chalky soil because it helps counteract the
alkalinity and holds moisture as well, but any of the substances
listed to improve sandy soil can be added to chalky soil with
good results.

'Acid' soils are those with a low lime content. Nearly all
plants are happy in them. Peaty soils contain a large proportion
of decaying vegetable matter and are very fertile, but they may
be so waterlogged that a large-scale drainage scheme is necessary before they can grow anything apart from bog plants.

The lime content of a soil is measured in what is known as
the pH scale. There is nothing abstruse about it and it is
simply a convenient yardstick, which tells us that any reading
above pH7 is alkaline and anything below it is acid. Various
soil-testing kits are available in the better gardening shops.

Good loam is the stuff that gardeners' dreams are made of,
being pleasant to work and capable of growing most plants. It
is a well-balanced mixture of sandy and clay soils combined
with decayed organic material and a very small proportion of
lime. Happily, continued cultivation and the addition of
animal manures, compost, leaf mould, and peat will gradually

improve the texture and fertility of most garden soils and make them more loamy.

DIGGING

The best way to prepare the soil for new plants is to dig it several weeks before they are due to arrive. It does not matter if the plants come later than expected, the important thing is to allow time for the dug soil to settle before planting takes place. Planting in newly dug ground is uncomfortable for the gardener, who soon finds he is working in a morass, and it is unsatisfactory for the plants, whose roots may be left in air pockets when the ground finally settles. When planting in soft, newly turned earth, too, it is difficult to finish up with a level surface over the whole border.

During digging perennial weeds should be carefully forked out and burnt. This will save a great deal of trouble later on, for, once the plants are in place, it is much more difficult to remove deep-rooting weeds. Weedkillers can be used certainly, but not without some risk among other plants, and, as the weedkillers cost a good deal of money, it is worth time removing every visible scrap of perennial weed when we have the chance.

Grass and annual weeds can be skimmed off with the spade and dug in. They must, however, be well buried and not simply turned over because we do not want them coming to the surface again during planting. This brings me to the subject of double digging.

Double digging means breaking up the soil to twice the depth of the spade, or two spits deep. I have listened to many arguments both for and against this procedure. Some gardeners think it a waste of time, others that it is essential for good cultivation. Most people agree that on heavy clay double digging should be done, because breaking up the subsoil helps drainage. The argument against double digging on light soils is that they are very well drained already and any further opening up of the soil only increases dryness and the speed with which plant foods are washed away. This is true if the ground is only being broken up and turned over, but I think myself that double digging of light soils is well worth the labour if bulky, moisture-retaining materials are available for digging into the subsoil.

If you decide to double-dig, this is how to go about it. At one end of the plot to be dug take out a trench two feet wide and the depth of your spade. Wheel this soil away to the other end of the plot. Returning to your starting point, step into the trench and fork up the soil, turning each forkful over, but

47. A winter-blooming evergreen shrub for acid soil, *Pieris japonica*

otherwise leaving it in the same position. Material for improving the drainage of heavy soil or the water-retaining properties of light soil should be forked into this broken-up earth at the bottom of the trench. Next dig another trench alongside and use the top soil from the second trench to fill in the first. Continue in this way, moving the top soil up one trench each time and forking the bottom soil over, until you reach the end of the plot. Finish by using the top soil brought from the first trench to fill in the last one.

ENRICHING THE SOIL

Well-rotted farmyard manure or compost, with granulated peat and bonemeal, may be added to the top twelve inches of soil during digging. Fresh, unrotted animal manures should not be used, as these damage plant roots instead of feeding them. A good proportion to use is half to one bucketful of manure or compost, a bucketful of peat, and four ounces of bonemeal to each square yard of ground. The peat must be damp before it is added to the soil. Peat holds water like a sponge and, used dry, it may not become saturated for months and can even steal water away from plant roots instead of helping to supply it.

Chapter Twelve

Planting and After-care of New Stock

Almost all planting is done in the autumn, winter, and very early spring, when soil in the open garden is more likely than not to be damp and sticky. While we are waiting for plants to be delivered it is a good idea to put a supply of fine soil under cover and to allow it to dry. At planting time this dry soil can be added to damp granulated peat at the rate of two parts soil to one of peat and the mixture sprinkled over the plants' roots as soon as they are in position. Successful planting depends very largely upon getting a plant's roots in close contact with the soil and this fine, almost dry mixture can be easily worked among the smallest roots to fill air pockets that might otherwise be left, causing roots to wither and rot.

Another small job that can be done in advance is to get stakes and ties ready to support new plants and to lay in a supply of sacks, polythene, and wire-netting to make windbreaks for delicate subjects.

WHAT TO DO WHEN PLANTS ARRIVE

Good nurserymen pack their plants with care and inside their protective wrappings plants can usually survive for about three weeks, so there is no need to panic if bad weather or any other circumstance prevents the planting of new stock immediately on its arrival.

If plants arrive when the soil is in workable condition, but when there is likely to be a considerable delay before there is time to plant them properly, they can be heeled in. To do this, dig a shallow, sloping trench in a vacant piece of ground, unwrap the plants completely and place their roots in the trench. Cover the roots with soil and tread it just sufficiently to make it firm.

Do not attempt either planting or heeling in when the ground is saturated or deeply frozen. Although having a supply of fine soil under cover means that planting is possible in very wet weather a good deal of tramping about on soggy ground is unavoidable while doing the job and this is very bad for the texture of the soil. It is better to wait for the ground to dry at least partially.

A thin layer of frost is another matter. If the crust of frosty soil is no more than an inch deep it can be skimmed off and heaped on one side to be spread on the surface again once planting is complete. Dealt with in this way, the frosty soil cannot do any harm to new plants.

When plants arrive during severe frost they should be put under cover and the bundles left closed. If it is available a frost-proof but unheated place is the best store, then, should the frost continue, we can unwrap the plants and dip their roots in a bucket of water each day. The plants should not stand in water all the time, however, and the roots should be well covered with straw or sacking except when they are being watered. Plants can be treated in the same way if the ground is waterlogged.

If they have to be stored for a time, do not unwrap the roots of 'balled' plants, that is, plants which have been despatched with their roots in a ball of soil wrapped in sacking or polythene. These are plants which resent root disturbance and the wrapping should not be taken off the soil ball until the plants are in their permanent positions and the roots are about to be covered with earth.

Then the covering can be loosened from the top and allowed to fall to the bottom of the planting hole. It is not necessary to pull it all out from beneath the plant as the roots will soon find their way through or round it, but the loose parts can be cut away before the hole is filled up with soil. Plants with 'balled' roots can survive a very long time out of the ground and they need only be placed in a frostproof shed and have their top growth uncovered if planting is likely to be long delayed.

SENSIBLE PLANTING

When several plants are to be put in they should be dealt with one at a time and the rest left under cover or with their roots well wrapped up to protect them from cold and drying winds until their turn comes. This is how to tackle the job. Examine the first plant and cut off any damaged roots. Look at the length of the roots, then dig a planting hole wide enough to take them at full stretch. Make the floor of the hole level or, better still, mound it up slightly towards the middle. This will prevent the roots being curled up and it will allow them to be spread out rather like the ribs of an umbrella so that they are in contact with the soil along their whole length. If the planting hole dips down in the middle it is easy to leave a dangerous air space under the centre of the plant. This space may fill with water and cause the roots to rot.

Plants should be replaced in the ground at the same level as before. There is usually a soil mark on the stems of shrubs and trees to guide us. The stems of herbaceous plants are bleached below ground level and change colour just where they break through the soil, so with this for a guide line they are quite easy to settle at the right depth. Climbing and bush roses should be planted with the point of budding one inch below ground level. This point is a swollen irregular lump low down on the stem. Check the depth of the planting hole by holding the plant in position and laying a cane close to it across the mouth of the hole. If the plant is at the right depth, the cane will touch the soil mark on the stem.

Tall shrubs and trees should be tied to a stake to prevent the wind blowing them over or rocking them back and forth before the roots have had a chance to anchor themselves. Hammer a stake into the hole and then put the plant in position with its main stem close to the support. Do not finish the planting and then bang in a stake. This way roots will almost certainly be damaged.

Once the right depth has been found, spread out the plant's roots and cover them by sprinkling in fine, dry soil or a mixture of soil and peat. Work the soil well in among the roots with the fingers to make sure that no air pockets are left. Once the roots are coated, begin to replace the soil taken from the planting hole. When the hole is about half-full grasp the plant firmly and gently ease it up and down several times to settle earth round its roots. Do not bump the plant about too vigorously, of course, just raise and lower it an inch or so. The soil round the plant can now be trodden on to firm it and then the rest of the hole should be filled in and the surface trodden again.

When the ground is dry, but not freezing, I like to give each plant a bucketful of water when the hole is half-filled in and has been trodden firm. In these circumstances I fill in the rest of the soil as soon as the water has disappeared but do not tread the surface until the following day.

Severe frost may loosen the ground round newly planted stock and when this happens the disturbed soil should be trodden firm again whenever it is noticed. If the soil is very soft and sticky a light sprinkling of dry peat or leaves on the surface will prevent too much of it clinging to the feet during this operation.

Do not use quick-acting fertilizers at planting time. They will not help the plants to establish themselves and may do them harm by scorching the roots. Bonemeal, on the other hand, is a slow-acting fertilizer which does nothing but good. If it has not already been added to the ground during digging, a handful can be sprinkled over the roots of each plant along with the soil and peat mixture.

PROTECTION AFTER PLANTING

I have already mentioned that tall specimens should be given supporting stakes and there are various ways of fixing the stems to these. Rubber ties are sold for the purpose in garden supply shops. These ties are very good because they do not cut into stems and can be adjusted as the plants grow. A cheaper tie can be made with tarred string, but this has a much shorter life and the stem to be supported must be protected with a strip of sacking or a piece of rubber to prevent the string biting into it.

While attending to the tying of new plants it is wise to examine the labels attached to them and if these are very tightly fastened to loosen the strings so that they cannot strangle the plants when growth begins.

In very windy positions young trees should be given extra support by driving a strut into the ground and nailing it to the upright stake at an angle of forty-five degrees. This strut can be put in place when planting has been completed.

When the weather is blustery, quite low unstaked shrubs may be rocked about until cup-shaped hollows form round their stems. These hollows should be filled in and firmed as soon as they are seen, otherwise they fill with water which may damage the plants, especially if it freezes.

The top growth of newly planted evergreens and all shrubs of doubtful hardiness can be given the protection of a sacking or polythene screen to shield it from the coldest winds and from driving rain and snow which can cause damage if it freezes on the branches of young stock. A screen slightly taller than the plant gives good shelter. It can be made from sacking stretched and tied over three or four stakes or angle irons thrust into the ground on the windward side of the plant and just clear of its root spread.

An alternative screening material is sheet polythene. This is cheap and it is easier for most gardeners to obtain than sacking. Because polythene tears easily and is apt to blow away it is best spread over a foundation of wire-netting and in very windy situations it can be sandwiched between two thicknesses of wire. Dried bracken roughly woven into wire-netting can also be used as a windbreak.

Small tender plants can be entirely enclosed in clear polythene bags pulled down to ground level over three or four short sticks set round the plant. Larger shrubs can be protected with a wigwam of clear polythene sheeting wrapped round a tripod of stakes and firmly tied where the stakes come together near the top. The lower edge of the polythene can be held in place with a few heavy stones or bricks. Although clear polythene allows light to pass through, plants also need a supply of air, so ventilation holes should always be punched in the sheeting when it is used to enclose plants completely.

All plants receive a shock when they are transplanted and it is more difficult for evergreens to withstand this shock than it is for deciduous subjects, because evergreens have to maintain foliage as well as roots at all times of year. The moist atmosphere inside a polythene cover can help them to do this. Newly planted evergreens which are not enclosed in polythene should be sprayed with water every few days in dry weather and spraying should be continued for at least a month after planting. As an alternative a spray can be bought to coat the foliage with a plastic material and retard the loss of moisture from leaf surfaces.

Silvery-leaved evergreens are the most difficult to protect. Plants in this class owe their colouring to the large numbers of hairs growing on their leaves and this kind of foliage is inclined to rot if it becomes waterlogged. For this reason silvery-leaved plants should not be enclosed in polythene as the moist atmosphere encourages mould to form on the leaves and rotting soon follows. The best help we can give is to make sure that such evergreens have a well-drained planting site in an open poisition where freely circulating air will help to dry the foliage quickly after rain. Panes of glass supported on short stakes can act as umbrellas over low growing plants in this class and will protect them from excessive rain without shutting them away from fresh air.

The roots of new stock can be protected from cold by spreading a thick layer of straw, granulated peat, or dead leaves over the ground immediately after planting. This dry material will stay in place inside a ring of wire-netting six to eight inches high. Without this wire barrier wind, birds, and domestic pets are apt to scatter the litter about and this results in a very untidy garden as well as depriving the plants of their protection.

It may sound topsy-turvy advice to buy plants for their winter beauty and then, during that very time, to hide them in unattractive swaddlings of one kind or another, but many shrubs and trees which are perfectly hardy once they are established need extra protection in their first season. No one wants to lose expensive plants and this extra care at the start usually means a better display in a shorter time.

PLANTING TIMES

Nurserymen can usually be relied upon to send out orders when the plants are unlikely to be harmed by the move. If they did not do this they would soon be out of business, thus there is seldom any need to worry when orders take a long time to arrive. When plants are in active growth the shock of being uprooted is very great and plants lifted at this time have a much slimmer chance of survival than those lifted during their dormant period. The dormant period for most plants is between October and April which is why the nurserymen send out most of their stocks at this time of year. After dry summers there is often some delay before the growers can begin despatching orders because plants cannot be lifted without damage until rain comes to soften the ground. Other delays occur during the severe frosts which put a stop to lifting operations just as effectually as to planting. Keeping these difficulties in mind it is better to wait patiently for our plants to arrive than to clamour for delivery and, provided an acknowledgement of the order has been received, to trust the nurseryman to do his best for us. All the same, it is useful to have some idea when to move different plants for then we can collect them from the gardens of friends with every chance of success and we can also move them safely from place to place in our own gardens.

Plants grown in pots or other portable containers suffer little root disturbance when they are moved. They can be transplanted successfully at almost any time of year provided we are sensible and avoid putting them in when the ground is deeply frozen or waterlogged in winter and if we water and spray them thoroughly and repeatedly after planting during hot dry summer weather.

Evergreen plants are the most difficult to move and re-establish because they are never completely dormant. This applies particularly to shrubs with a considerable amount of foliage to support and when new specimens appear to have a poor root system it lessens the strain on the plant if some of the top growth is shortened to give the roots less work. The safest times for planting evergreens are said to be in early October or late April but if the ground happens to be saturated just then it is much more sensible to wait a bit until the soil is more workable and to be guided by local conditions rather than the calendar.

Most hardy herbaceous plants and deciduous shrubs with fibrous wiry roots can be safely moved at any time once growth slows down. This dormant period begins in autumn, when the yellowing and dropping of leaves are signs that sap pressure is flagging, and continues until just before new growth starts in spring. Plants on the borderline of hardiness and those with thick fleshy roots are not so accommodating. They are best moved in early spring when the chances are that the temperature will soon rise and enable growth to start. If this type of plant is moved in autumn or winter its roots may rot during their long wait for warmer conditions.

People who garden on light sandy soil can take greater risks in moving plants than those who have heavy or badly drained ground to contend with. Light soils are the warmest and plants moved in the autumn can usually take hold and make some root growth before severe weather makes them completely dormant. Even in the depths of winter new stock is seldom harmed in well-drained soil. In heavy and badly drained soils, on the other hand, growth comes to a standstill much earlier and dormant plants can be chilled, if not drowned outright. In these soils winter planting is better avoided and whenever possible plants should be moved in early spring.

I have already mentioned that local conditions are a better guide to planting times than the calendar, and in my own garden, on fairly light ground, I have moved plants success-fully at all times of year and in all weathers except severe frost. Plants which are moved from one part of the garden to another have an easier time, of course, than those we receive from a distance. They spend so short a time out of the ground and it is possible to lift and move them with a good deal of

48. Female plants of two berrying evergreens, *Skimmia japonica* (left)
and *Viburnum davidii*

soil clinging to their roots. The advantage of this is that the
fine root hairs suffer little damage during transplanting and
can go straight on with their job of nourishing the plant. To
make sure that soil will remain round the roots when they are
lifted in dry weather, the plants to be moved should be very
thoroughly watered the previous day. If the plants are then
put in carefully and firmly and if they are kept well supplied
with water for some weeks after the move they should go
right ahead with very few signs of disturbance even in the
height of summer.

Chapter Thirteen

Some Tasks for the Winter Gardener

Dead leaves enrich the ground but in the garden we cannot let them drift around just as they fall. To begin with, dead leaves make the garden look uncared for, but there are more important reasons for gathering them up. Not all the small plants we grow are at home in woodland and those which are not can be killed if they are buried under leaves during the winter. Alpine plants in particular are unfitted to cope with a sodden covering of this kind and, because we so often grow them in pockets where dead leaves can easily accumulate, a tidying up of the rockery is one of the most essential jobs in the autumn garden. Lawn sweeping is another important chore because grass, too, dies if it is cut off from light and air, while wet leaves on stone or concrete paths are treacherous underfoot.

Another reason for gathering up dead leaves is to prevent slugs, snails, woodlice, or any other garden pest from finding cosy winter quarters among them. Weeds and cultivated annuals which have completed their cycle of growth should also be cleared away before they become havens for slugs and snails and to prevent plant diseases from overwintering on them.

Some gardeners like to shear away all the fading top growth from their herbaceous perennials in autumn for the sake of neatness, but from the plant's point of view this is not a very good idea, as it means their crowns are unprotected during the winter. The indiscriminate removal of all the top growth from these plants also destroys one of the beauties of the winter garden, shapely seed heads bleached by the weather and, when we are specially favoured, covered with hoar frost.

Plants like the sea hollies, whose top growth is woody and decorative, can be left to entertain us in this way while those with no great claims to beauty can be trimmed down to within eight inches of the ground and this stubble of stems will shelter the roots and dormant crowns of the plants without looking untidy.

COMPOST MAKING

Farmyard and stable manures become dearer and scarcer all the time, but compost made from waste plant material is a very good substitute. With the exception of diseased plants, woody stems, and the strong roots of such persistent weeds as docks and bindweeds, all vegetable matter can safely by made into compost and returned to the soil as food material. Compost making can go on all the year round but it receives a boost when the dead leaves are swept up and the borders are tidied in autumn. Kitchen waste can be composted too and is a considerable help when there is only a small garden from which to collect material. Animal manures can be added to the heap and will hasten the rotting process, but they are not essential; garden chemicals can be used instead. There are also several proprietary compost activators on the market and these make good compost when they are used according to the makers' instructions.

The normal way to make a compost heap is to build it up in layers on bare ground and it should be three to four feet square, as smaller heaps do not decompose well. The heap is easily controlled and kept tidy if it is enclosed on three sides with wire netting fixed to corner posts or, alternatively, it can be built up inside an open-fronted bunker.

To make a compost heap, begin with damp plant material and tread this down into a firm layer about nine inches thick, next add a two-inch layer of animal manure, then a two-inch layer of soil. Build up the heap by repeating these layers until a height of four to five feet has been reached. When no animal manure is available the compost will still be satisfactory if the vegetable layer is sprinkled with sulphate of ammonia and the soil layer with lime. To make sure the heap is uniformly damp each layer of vegetable refuse can be watered as it is completed.

When the heap has reached its full height it should be covered with polythene to conserve moisture and the heat generated by the decomposing material. The outside of the heap usually remains more or less unchanged but in two or three months, depending on the time of year, all the rest should have turned into rich brown crumbly material which is ideal either as a mulch or for digging into the soil. When the time comes to use the prepared compost the outer crust of the heap can be sliced off and set aside to make the first layer of a new heap.

GARDEN FURNITURE IN WINTER

Once we have achieved a garden that looks attractive in winter it is pleasant to sit out and enjoy it on fine days. Lightweight garden chairs are useful at all times of year because they can be kept under cover and carried outside when the sun shines. Metal- or wooden-framed canvas chairs are easy to move about and so is wicker furniture. My own favourite is a hooded wicker armchair which is very comfortable and has only to be turned in the right direction to shade my eyes from the sun or my back from the wind.

Apart from mobile garden furniture, we may want heavier kinds which can be left out in all weathers without deteriorating. Soft-wood seats can be treated with special priming paint made to protect horticultural woodwork, before being finished off with any hard gloss paint sold for exterior decorating. They can also be coated with a thick varnish to resist damp. Both teak and elm furniture is weather resistant and needs no painting, although teak will benefit from a coating of linseed oil if it has been very much dried out by the sun. Elm needs no coating and weathers to a soft silvery-grey colour.

Cast-aluminium furniture is also completely weatherproof, but its paint may need renewing after a winter out of doors. This furniture is being produced both in new designs and in old ones covered with scrolls and curlicues copied from the cast-iron furniture it resembles. Painted white, it looks very attractive among flowers or evergreens.

ICE AND SNOW HAZARDS

Ice is unlikely to damage a garden pool whose sides slope outwards at the top but if the sides go straight up or slope inwards the pool may be cracked by the pressure of trapped ice. The risk of this happening can be reduced by floating hollow rubber balls on the water in winter because these will give when ice forms and reduce the strain on the sides of the pool.

Another frost danger threatens not the pool but fish kept in it. When the water is completely frozen over, poisonous gases cannot escape and may kill the fish. These gases rise continually from decaying vegetable matter in the water but normally do no harm. If we bang a hole in the ice each time it forms, the gases disperse but vibrations from repeated blows can injure the fish, so it is better to make a hole by pouring hot water on to the ice. If there is an electricity supply for running a fountain in the pool during the summer this can be connected to a small immersion heater in severe weather and a patch of water kept free from ice. Suitable heaters are stocked by shops selling equipment for tropical fish tanks.

Plants we know to be frost tender can be protected by any of the methods suggested in Chapter Twelve or, if they are small enough, by being covered with cloches.

Snow does not do a great deal of harm in the garden and when icy winds are blowing a snow covering is a good protection for plants in the open borders. Ornamental trees and shrubs, however, may be damaged if snow is left on their branches. Evergreens are the chief sufferers. After heavy snow has fallen it pays to go round the garden with a long-handled broom to knock snow from laden branches and the tops of hedges before they become permanently bent or broken.

LAWN CARE IN WINTER

Lawns usually emerge none the worse when snow melts, but patches of compacted snow may be slow to thaw and can do damage to the grass, so when snow is being cleared from paths it should be broadcast or piled on borders rather than on lawns. For the same reason it is better if children can be induced to build their snowmen on a bare patch of ground or a paved area instead of on the grass.

But it is the exception rather than the rule for our lawns to be covered with snow in winter and when the weather is good we can do quite a lot to keep them in trim. After the grass has been cut for the last time in autumn, the mower should be sent to be sharpened because at this time of year it will be dealt with much more promptly than during the spring rush.

When the fallen leaves have been swept up, lawns benefit from a good raking to remove dead growth, followed by spiking to aerate the soil. On small lawns these jobs can be done with a wire rake and an ordinary border fork, for large areas power tools can be bought. If a dressing of sand, peat, and lawn fertilizer is then scattered all over the surface and brushed in the lawn will need no more feeding until early spring.

Another task to do in good winter weather is the minor plastic surgery of levelling out bumps and dips which are spoiling the surface of the lawn. To level a raised patch, first remove the turf with a sharp spade, skim off the unwanted soil, then lightly fork up the earth below before replacing the turf. This helps the grass roots to take hold again quickly. In the same way, fork up the bottom of a depression after removing the turf and before adding more soil. Leave the finished surface of the patches a little above the level of the surrounding turf to allow for the soil settling again.

A broken grass edge can be straightened without reducing the size of the lawn if the damaged turf is lifted and turned round so that the strong newly-cut edge is placed at the outside and the broken part towards the centre of the lawn. The flaw caused by the broken edge can be filled in with good soil and sown with grass seed in spring. Any other small bare patches in the body of the lawn can be forked up and, if necessary, levelled with extra soil ready for re-sowing at the same time.

New lawns can be turfed in winter or the site prepared for raising a lawn from seed sown in the spring. Whichever way the lawn is to be made, the preliminary digging of the site is the same, with particular attention being paid to drainage, because grass cannot do well in waterlogged soil. After the ground has had time to settle it must be made very firm by treading and shortly before turf is laid or seed is sown a general fertilizer should be raked into the top soil.

If the ground is firm and level and the turves are all the same thickness, a smooth surface to the lawn is guaranteed. To check the thickness of the turves each one can be laid grass side down in a shallow box and any excess soil above the box sliced away with a knife. It saves work later on to examine each turf at the same time and to pull out big weeds like plaintains. To lay the lawn, turves are put down in rows with the joints in each row bonded like brickwork. When all are in place the new lawn should be very lightly rolled before fine soil is scattered over it and brushed into the joints to help them knit together.

KEEPING THE BIRDS ALIVE

Some people argue that to help birds survive and increase is simply to load the dice against ourselves in our efforts to create a colourful garden. It is undeniable that birds can do a lot of damage by stripping off flower buds and eating fruit, but, as they also eat large numbers of aphids and other insect pests, the argument is not entirely one-sided. Because their livelihood is at stake, professional plant breeders and fruit growers take stringent measures to keep birds down, but most of us who garden for pleasure like to see birds flitting about and consider that the sight and sound of them compensates for the loss of some of our autumn berries.

But, although we decide to feed and protect birds in the garden, we need not be entirely passive when they get up to mischief. Black cotton criss-crossed among branches and over low-growing plants will protect our choicest early flowers and is quite invisible, so it does nothing to mar the appearance of the garden. Black cotton has several advantages over repellent sprays. It is unaffected by rain and does no harm to the gardener, the plants, or the birds.

During the winter when their natural food is scarce we must do more than merely allow birds the freedom of the garden. If we want them to survive we must feed them regularly and see that they have drinking water during frosty weather.

The first thing to remember is that birds are frightened by changes and take some time to become accustomed to any new object in the garden, so feeding should begin before the severe weather starts. Once a routine has been established and birds are coming to a table, a water dish, or other feeders, we should keep these in the same places and, if it is possible, put out some food and water every day all through the winter and until the spring frosts are over.

To keep it safe from cats, a bird-table should be placed on a pole at least four feet high or suspended by chains from a tree. Not all wild birds will eat from a table, however, so a tray on the ground is also useful. This is better than scattering scraps directly on the ground because a tray of uneaten food can be taken indoors at night and does not encourage rats and mice. The birds who like to cling while feeding can be catered for with wire-mesh cages filled with scraps and hung from hooks below a feeding table, on the outside of a window frame, or from a tree.

Most table scraps are relished by birds when natural food is scarce and fat is particularly useful to them in cold weather. Too much bread is not good but stale cake, cheese rinds, damaged apples, meaty bones, and left-over potatoes, porridge, or puddings are all nourishing foods which cost us nothing. If we can add to these some shelled nuts, a coconut sawn in two and a few of the mixed seeds sold for wild birds our garden visitors will do very nicely.

When nights are frosty but the day temperature rises above freezing, it is sufficient to put out water in the mornings and to

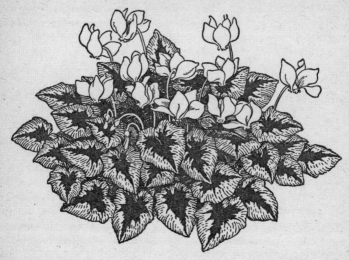

49. An autumn-blooming plant, *Cyclamen neapolitanum* 'Album'

make sure the dishes are free from ice in the late afternoon so that birds can drink before going to roost. In very severe weather we can prevent drinking water freezing during the day by putting a dish on top of a saucepan of hot water but this, of course, does not keep warm for very long and has to be refilled several times a day. Alternatively, we can place the water dish on a triangle of three bricks and burn an eight-hour nightlight beneath it.

Index